Junior
Worldmark
Encyclopedia of

World Holidays

Junior Worldmark Encyclopedia of World Holidays

VOLUME 3

Hanukkah,
Independence Day,
Kwanzaa

AN IMPRINT OF THE GALE GROUP

DETROIT · NEW YORK · SAN FRANCISCO
LONDON · BOSTON · WOODBRIDGE, CT

Junior Worldmark Encyclopedia of World Holidays

Robert H. Griffin and Ann H. Shurgin

Staff

Kelle Sisung, *Contributing Editor*
Carol DeKane Nagel, *U·X·L Managing Editor*
Thomas L. Romig, *U·X·L Publisher*
Meggin Condino, *Senior Analyst, New Product Development*

Dean Dauphinais, *Senior Editor, Imaging and Multimedia Content*
Shalice Shah-Caldwell, *Permissions Associate, Text and Pictures*

Robert Duncan, *Senior Imaging Specialist*
Randy A. Bassett, *Image Database Supervisor*
Barbara J. Yarrow, *Graphic Services Manager*

Pamela A. E. Galbreath, *Senior Art Director*
Graphix Group, *Typesetting*

Rita Wimberley, *Senior Buyer*
Evi Seoud, *Assistant Manager, Composition Purchasing and Electronic Prepress*
Dorothy Maki, *Manufacturing Manager*

Printed in the United States of America
10 9 8 7 6 5 4 3 2 1

Library of Congress Cataloging-in-Publication Data

Junior worldmark encyclopedia of world holidays/ edited by Robert Griffin.
   p.   cm.
Includes bibliographical references and index.
Summary: Alphabetically arranged entries provide descriptions of celebrations around the world of some thirty holidays and festivals, including national and cultural holidays, such as Independence Day and New Year's Day, which are commemorated on different days for different reasons in a number of countries.
ISBN 0-7876-3927-3 (set). — ISBN 0-7876-3928-1 (vol. 1). — ISBN 0-7876-3929-X (vol. 2). — ISBN 0-7876-3930-3 (vol. 3). — ISBN 0-7876-3931-1 (vol. 4).
1. Holidays—Encyclopedias, Juvenile. 2. Festivals—Encyclopedias, Juvenile. [1. Holidays—Encyclopedias. 2. Festivals—Encyclopedias. 3. Encyclopedias and dictionaries.] I. Griffin, Robert H., 1951–

GT3933 .J86 2000
394.26'03—dc21

                                    00-023425

Front cover photographs (top to bottom): Krewe of Rex float reproduced by permission of Archive Photos, Inc; jack-o-lanterns, monk beating drum, and Fastnacht witches reproduced by permission of AP/Wide World Photos, Inc. Back cover photograph: Chicago Children's Choir reproduced by permission of AP/Wide World Photos, Inc.

Contents

Contents

Volume 3:

Volume 4:

Contents
by Country

Contents by Country

Reader's Guide

Ever wonder why children trick-or-treat on Halloween? How Christmas festivities in Italy differ from those in the United States? What the colors of Kwanzaa represent? When will Ramadan come this year? Who creates all those floats in the parades? The answers to these and other questions about holiday traditions and lore can be found in *Junior Worldmark Encyclopedia of World Holidays*. This four-volume set explores when, where, why, and how people from thirty countries around the world celebrate eleven different holidays.

Each chapter in *Junior Worldmark Encyclopedia of World Holidays* opens with a general overview of the featured holiday. The chapter then provides details on one to six countries that observe that holiday. Each overview and country profile is arranged into the following rubrics, allowing for quick scanning or comparisons among the countries and holidays:

- **Introduction:** Offers a brief description and useful background information on the holiday. The introduction in the overview discusses the holiday in general; the country introductions focus on how the holiday is observed in that featured country.

- **History:** Discusses the holiday's development, often from ancient origins through modern times. When a holiday was established to commemorate a historical event, such as a revolution or a nation's declaration of independence, a historical account of the event is given. When a holiday began with the rise of a religion, a discussion of the growth of the religion follows. Each holiday's general history is presented in the overview, while its development in a particular country is the focus of the country history.

- **Folklore, Legends, Stories:** Each holiday has at least a few legends and stories, folklore and superstitions associated with it. These are discussed here, along with literature commonly associated with the holiday. Traditional characters or historical tales can be found, as well as a brief synopsis of a well-known story or an excerpt from a poem. Religious holidays include excerpts or synopses of the scriptural account on which they are based. For some holidays, sidebars listing popular stories and poems are included.

- **Customs, Traditions, Ceremonies:** This section delves into the actual celebration of the holiday, from preparation for its arrival through ceremonies to bid it farewell for another year. Some of the ceremonies and traditions are religious, others are secular. Some are based on beliefs and superstitions so old that no one knows their origin, while others center around the reenactment of historical or religious events. Some are carried out on a grand scale, while others involve a quiet family ceremony. Learn how a European family celebrates a particular holiday while someone in Africa or Asia celebrates it in a very different—or sometimes very similar—way.

- **Clothing, Costumes:** Some holidays, such as Halloween and Carnival, have costumes at the heart of the celebration. For others, such as Independence Days, simply wearing the national colors is enough. In many cultures, people don traditional folk costumes for particular holidays, while others just dress in their "Sunday best." Whether it is a pair of sneakers or a six-foot feather plume, clothing and costumes play an important role in the traditions. This section will explain how people dress for the holiday and why.

- **Foods, Recipes:** What does Christmas dinner mean to an Italian family? What do Chinese youngsters snack on at New Year festivals? What is the main "Thanksgiving dinner" dish in Swaziland? This rubric details the special holiday meals shared by people within a culture. It covers the foods themselves as well as table settings, mealtime ceremonies, and the significance of eating certain foods on special days. For some holidays, picnic or festival foods are also mentioned. For most countries, a favorite holiday recipe is featured.

- **Arts, Crafts, Games:** Described here are famous works of art associated with specific holidays, as well as crafts created by different peoples in connection with the holiday, such as intricate Nativity scenes made by Italian woodcarvers and special pictures created by Chinese artists to bring good luck in the New Year. Holiday decorations and traditional games are also discussed here. Included for some holidays are crafts projects that, in addition to bringing added enjoyment by making one's own decorations, will help foster an appreciation of the art of other cultures.

- **Symbols:** Included in the holiday overviews are discussions of the symbols associated with the holiday and its celebration. A description of each symbol is given, along with its origin, meaning, and significance to the holiday.

- **Music, Dance:** Whether performing classical compositions or folk dancing in a courtyard, people all over the world love to make music and dance during their holidays. This rubric focuses on the music and dance that helps make up holiday celebrations. Some musical performances can be fiercely competitive, like the steel band contests held during Carnival in Trinidad. Others are solemn and deeply moving, like a performance of Handel's *Messiah* in a cathedral at Easter. Here learn about folk instruments, the origins of songs and dances, and famous composers or musicians from many cultures. Excerpts from songs associated with the holiday are also given.

- **Special Role of Children, Young Adults:** Children and young adults often have a special role to play in holiday celebrations. While children may simply participate in family activities during a holiday in some countries, in others children have distinct roles in parades, plays and performances, or customs. Here students can learn how children their own age celebrate holidays in nations thousands of miles away.

- **For More Information and Sources:** Print and electronic sources for further study are found at the end of each holiday overview and again at the end of each country essay. Those following the overview are general sources for the holiday, whereas the others pertain to a particular nation. Books listed should be able to be found in a library, and electronic sources are accessible on the World Wide Web.

Additionally, each chapter contains a Holiday Fact Box highlighting the themes of the specific holiday, while sprinkled throughout the set are boxes featuring recipes, activities, and more fascinating facts. One hundred twenty-five photos help bring the festivities to life. Beginning each volume is a table of contents for the entire set listing the holidays and countries featured, a table of contents by country, an explanation of how the modern calendar

developed, a calendar list of world holidays, and a words to know section. Concluding each volume is a cumulative subject index providing easy access to the holidays, countries, traditions, and topics discussed throughout *Junior Worldmark Encyclopedia of World Holidays*.

Advisory Board

Special thanks to the *Junior Worldmark Encyclopedia of World Holidays* advisors for their invaluable comments and suggestions:

- Mary Alice Anderson, Media Specialist, Winona Middle School, Winona, Minnesota.

- Ginny Ayers, Department Chair, Media Technology Services, Evanston Township High School, Evanston, Illinois.

- Jonathan Betz-Zall, Children's Librarian, Sno-Isle Regional Library System, Edmonds, Washington.

- Peter Butts, Media Specialist, East Middle School, Holland, Michigan.

Comments and Suggestions

We welcome your comments on this work as well as your suggestions for holidays to be featured in future editions of *Junior Worldmark Encyclopedia of World Holidays*. Please write: Editors, *Junior Worldmark Encyclopedia of World Holidays*, U•X•L, 27500 Drake Rd., Farmington Hills, MI 48331–3535; call toll-free: 1–800–877–4253; fax: 248–414–5043; or send e-mail via www.galegroup.com.

How the Modern Calendar Developed

The Egyptian Calendar

The earliest known calendar, that of the Egyptians, was lunar based, or calculated by the cycles of the Moon. One cycle is a lunar month, about 29.5 days in length, the time it takes the Moon to revolve once around the Earth. Although the calculations are fairly simple, reliance upon lunar months eventually leads to a problem: a lunar year, based upon 12 lunar cycles, is only 354 days. This is 11 days shorter than the solar year, the time it takes Earth to revolve once around the Sun. In any agricultural society, such as that of ancient Egypt, the solar-based seasons of the year are vitally important: they are the most reliable guide for knowing when to plow, plant, harvest, or store agricultural produce. Obviously, the discrepancy between the lunar and solar year had to be addressed.

The Egyptian solution was to rely on a solar calendar to govern civil affairs and agriculture; this was put in place around the third millennium B.C. This calendar observed the same new year's day as the older lunar one, which for the Egyptians was the day, about July 3, of the appearance on the horizon just before sunrise of the star Sirius, the "Dog Star." This event was significant for the Egyptians, for it occurred at nearly the same time the Nile River flooded each year, the key to their agricultural prosperity. The new Egyptian solar calendar also retained the division of days into months, although they were no longer based on lunar cycles. The Egyptian year in the reformed calendar contained 12 months of 30 days, with 5 days added throughout the year, bringing the total number of days to 365. It was only a fraction of a day different from the length of the solar year as determined by modern scientific means.

The Sumerian Calendar

Like the early Egyptian calendar, the ancient Sumerian calendar, developed around the twenty–seventh century B.C., was lunar. To the Sumerians, however, the Moon's cycles were apparently more significant, for they retained lunar months and a 354–day year. They made alignments with the seasons by adding extra days outside the regular calendar. (This process of adding extra days as necessary to reconcile the lunar with the solar year is called intercalation.) The calendar of the sacred city of Nippur, which became the Sumerian standard in the eighteenth century B.C., assigned names to the months, with the intercalary month designated by royal decree.

The Seven–day Week

The ancient Babylonians, a Sumerian people with a highly developed astronomy, are thought to be the first people to observe a seven-day week. The concept was probably based upon the periods between the distinct phases of the moon, which roughly correspond to seven days. The Babylonians also regarded the number seven as sacred, probably because they knew of seven principal heavenly bodies—Sun, Moon, Mars, Mercury, Jupiter, Venus, and Saturn—and saw supernatural significance in their seemingly wild movements against a backdrop of fixed stars. The days of the week were named for these principal heavenly bodies, one assigned to each day according to which governed the first hour of that day.

In addition to their lunar calendar, the Babylonians also devised a solar calendar based upon the points at which the Sun rises in relation to the constellations. This calendar is the basis for the zodiac system, the key to astrology.

From the Babylonians, the ancient Hebrews are believed to have adopted the practices of intercalation and observance of a seven-day week, probably during the time of Jewish captivity in Babylon beginning in 586 B.C. Babylonian influence may also have played a role in their observing every seventh day as special—the Jewish concept of Sabbath. Evidence for an earlier Jewish calendar (from at least the twelfth century B.C.)

does exist, however; thus, the observance of a Sabbath may well have existed before the Babylonian captivity. In any event, it is clear that the tradition of the seven-day week, as well as the retention of the concept of months, has much to do with the Western inheritance of Jewish calendar practices. (See also **The Hebrew Calendar**, below.)

The seven-day week as we know it today was carried into Christian use in the first century A.D. and was officially adopted by the Roman emperor Constantine in the fourth century. Interestingly, the English names for the days still reflect their origin in the names of the seven principal heavenly bodies of the ancient Babylonian astronomy:

- **Sunday:** Old English *Sunnan daeg*, a translation of Latin *dies solis*, "day of the sun."

- **Monday:** Old English *Monan daeg*, a translation of Latin *lunae dies*, "day of the moon"; compare with the French *lundi*.

- **Tuesday:** Old English *Tiwes daeg*, "day of Tiw," an adaptation of Latin *dies Martis*, "day of Mars" (the god Tiw being identified with the Roman Mars); compare with the French *Mardi*.

- **Wednesday:** Old English *Wodnes daeg*, "Woden's Day," an adaptation of Latin *Mercurii dies*, "day of Mercury" (the god Woden being identified with the Roman Mercury); compare with the French *mercredi*.

- **Thursday:** Old English *Thunres daeg*, "Thunor's day" or "Thor's day," an adaptation of the Latin *dies Jovis*, "day of Jove" (the god Thor being identified with the Roman Jove); compare with the French *jeudi*.

- **Friday:** Old English *Frize daeg*, "Freya's Day," an adaptation of the Latin *dies Veneris*, "day of Venus" (the goddess Freya being identified with the Roman Venus); compare with the French *vendredi*.

- **Saturday:** Old English *Saetern(es) daeg*, derived from the Latin *Saturni Dies*, "day of Saturn."

The Hebrew Calendar

Little is known of the Hebrew calendar prior to the Exodus from Egypt (c. 1250 B.C.) except that it appears to have contained four single and four double months called *yereah*. The early Hebrews apparently did not study the heavens and timekeeping as did their Sumerian and Egyptian neighbors. In fact, it was only after the period of Babylonian exile (586–516 B.C.) that a more fully developed method of timekeeping was adopted to modify the ancient practices. After their return from captivity, the Hebrews employed a calendar very similar to that of the Babylonians, intercalating (adding as necessary) months into the lunar calendar so it would correspond with the solar year. Unlike the Babylonians, who marked the beginning of the new year in the spring, the Hebrews retained the custom of recognizing the new year in the autumn, the time of their principal religious festivals of Rosh Hashanah (New Year), Yom Kippur, the Sukkoth, all falling in the month of Tishri (September/October). Still, similarities between the Jewish and Babylonian calendars are clear from a comparison of the names used in each system for the months:

Names of the Months in the Babylonian and Jewish Calendar Systems

Babylonian	Jewish	Equivalent
Nisanu	Nisan	March/April
Aiaru	Iyar	April/May
Simanu	Sivan	May/June
Du'uzu	Tammuz	June/July
Abu	Ab	July/August
Ululu	Elul	August/September
Tashritu	Tishri	September/October
Arahsamnu	Heshvan	October/November
Kislimu	Kislev	November/December
Tebetu	Tebet	December/January
Shabatu	Shebat	January/February
Adaru I	Adar	February/March
Adaru II	Veadar	(intercalary)

Thus, the year in the Jewish (and Babylonian) calendar consists of 12 lunar months, with the addition of the intercalary month as necessary to synchronize with the solar year. The months contain alternately 29 or 30 days; the beginning of each is marked by the appearance of the new moon.

The Hebrew week ends with the observation of the Sabbath, lasting from sunset Friday to sunset Saturday, a day to rest and pay homage to God. The use of weeks and observation of a day of rest are primarily contributions from Jewish tradition to our present–day calendar. (See also **The Seven–day Week**, above.)

The Jewish Era, designated *A.M.* (for Latin *anno mundi*, "year of the world"), begins with the supposed date of Creation, which tradition sets at 3761 B.C. After more than two thousand years, devout Jews still observe essentially the same calendar for religious purposes, although they follow other calendars for their business and social lives. With its roots based in scripture, the Hebrew calendar has remained a primary binding force of tradition and continuity throughout the long and varied history of the Jewish people.

The Early Roman Calendar

Ancient Rome played a significant role in the development of our modern method of reckoning time. The earliest known Roman calendar, created according to legend by the city's founder, Romulus, in the eighth century B.C., had 10 months totaling 304 days: 6 months of 30 days and 4 months of 31 days. The new year began in March, the time when agricultural activities were revived and new military campaigns were initiated, and ended with December, which was followed by a winter gap that was used for intercalation. The Etruscan king Numa Pompilius (reigned 715–673 B.C.) reformed Romulus's primitive calendar, instituting a lunar year of 12 months. The two new months, following December, were named *Januarius* and *Februarius,* and were respectively assigned 29 and 28 days.

While this reform was a clear improvement, it was set aside in Rome during a time of political unrest that began about 510 B.C. Still, its advantages were remembered, and in 153 B.C. Numa Pompilius's calendar was again adopted. At the same time the beginning of the Roman civil year was changed to January 1, which became the day that newly elected consuls assumed office.

Days of the Roman Month

The Romans did not have a method for numbering the days of their months in a series. They did, however, establish three fixed points from which other days could be reckoned. These three designations were: 1) *Kalends,* the first day of the month (ancestor of English *calendar*); 2) *Nones,* the ninth day; and 3) *Ides,* originally the day of the full moon of the lunar month. In months of 31 days (March, May, July, October) the Nones were the seventh day and the Ides the fifteenth, while in the shorter months the Nones fell on the fifth and the Ides on the thirteenth day.

The Romans also recognized a market day, called *nundinae,* which occurred every eighth day. This established a cycle for agriculture in which the farmer worked for seven days in his field and brought his produce to the city on the eighth for sale.

The Julian Calendar

It was not until the mid-first century B.C., by which time the reformed lunar calendar had shifted eight weeks out of phase with the seasons, that emperor Julius Caesar determined that a long-term and scientific reform of the calendar must take place. He enlisted the aid of the Alexandrian astronomer Sosigenes to devise the new calendar. The solar year was reckoned quite accurately at 365.25, and the calendar provided for years of 365 days with an additional day in February every fourth year. In 46 B.C. a total of 90 days were intercalated into the year, bringing the calendar back into phase with the seasons. As a result, what would have been March 1, 45 B.C. was, in the new system, referred to as January 1, 45 B.C. Thus 46 B.C. was a long year, containing 445 days, and was referred to by Romans as *ultimus annus confusionis,* "the last year of the muddled reckoning."

In 10 B.C. it was found that the priests in charge of administering the new Roman calendar had wrongly intercalated the extra day every third year rather than every fourth. In order to rectify the situation, the emperor Augustus declared that no 366–day years should be observed for the next 12 years, and made certain that future intercalation would be properly conducted. With this minor adjustment, the Julian calendar was fully in place, so to remain for the next 1,626 years.

The Gregorian Calendar

Since the Julian calendar year of 365.25 days (averaging in the leap-year day) was slightly longer than the actual length of a solar year, 365.242199 days, over time even this system proved wanting, growing out of phase by about three or four days every four centuries. By the time of Pope Gregory XIII in the late sixteenth century, the difference between the calendar and the seasons had grown to ten days; the vernal equinox of 1582 occurred on March 11. Left without change, the Julian calendar would have resulted in fixed holy days occurring in the "wrong" season, which bewildered church officials. Moreover, certain fixed holy days were also used to determine when to plant and harvest crops.

Pope Gregory's reform, presented in the papal bull of February 24, 1582, consisted of deleting ten days from the year (the day following October 5 was designated as October 15) and declaring that three out of every four "century" years (1700, 1800, etc.) would not be leap years; if a century year, such as 1600, were divisible by 400, it would be a leap year. These modifications established the form of our present calendar.

In spite of its superior accuracy, the Gregorian calendar met with resistance in various parts of the world, and was not used until the eighteenth century in Protestant Europe and the American colonies, and even later still in areas under strong Byzantine influence.

Although the Gregorian calendar measures out a year that is slightly longer than the solar year (differing by about 25 seconds a year, or 3 days in every 10,000 years) its general workability and accuracy have led to its use worldwide for nearly all nonreligious purposes.

Calendar of Holidays

January

January 1
New Year's Day
Solemnity of Mary the Mother of God

January 1 or 2
St. Basil's Day

January 2
Second New Year

January 5–6
Epiphany Eve and Epiphany
Twelfth Night
Day of the Three Kings/Día de los Tres Reyes

First Monday after Twelfth Day
Plough Monday

January 6 or 7
Old Christmas

January 7
Gannā
St. Distaff's Day
St. John the Baptist's Day

January 11
St. Brictiva's Day

January 12
Old New Year's Day

January 12–15
Festival of Our Lord Bonfim

January 13
St. Knut's Day
Old Silvester

January 14
Magh Sankranti

January 15
Pilgrimage to the Shrine of the Black Christ
Adult's Day

January 16
St. Honoratus's Day

January 19 and 20
Timqat (Epiphany) and St. Michael's Feast

January 20
St. Sebastian's Day
St. Agnes Eve

January 21
St. Sarkis's Day

January 22
St. Dominique's Day (Midwife's Day)
St. Vincent's Day

January 24
Festival of Abundance

January 25
Burns Night

Last Tuesday in January
Up Helly Aa

Fifteenth Day, Shevat (January–February)
Tu Bi-Shevat (Fifteenth Day, Shevat)

Month of Magha (January–February)
Urn Festival

Month of Tagu, Days 1–4
Thingyan

Last Month, Last Day of Lunar Year
New Year's Eve

Moon 1, Days 1–15
New Year

Moon 1, Day 1
Tibetan New Year (Losar)

Moon 1, First Two Weeks (circa February)
Prayer Festival

Moon 1, Day 7
Festival of the Seven Grasses

Moon 1, Day 9
Making Happiness Festival

Moon 1, Days 14–19 (circa February)
Butter Sculpture Offering Festival

Moon 1, Day 15
Great Fifteenth
Burning of the Moon House Festival
Lantern Festival
Birthday of the Great Emperor–Official
of the Heavens

Moon 1, Day 16
Sixteenth Day

Moon 1, Day 19
Rats' Wedding Day

January–February
Rice Festival

Thai/Tai
Thai Poosam

February

Circa February
Tsagan Sara (New Year)

February
Clean Tent Ceremony
Winterlude

February 1
St. Brigid's Day

February 1–3 (circa)
Setsubun

February 2
Candlemas/Candelaria
Feast of the Virgin of the Suyapa
Queen of Waters Festival

February 3, 5
St. Blaise's Day, St. Agatha's Day

February 5
Igbi

February 10
Feast of St. Paul's Shipwreck

February 11
St. Vlasios's Day

February–March (Day 10 of Dhu'l-hija)
Id Al-Kabir (The Great Feast)

Moveable: February–March (Sunday before Lent)
Cheese Sunday

Moveable: February–March
Shrove Monday
Shrove Tuesday/Mardi Gras
Carnival
Ash Wednesday

Moveable: February–March (First Sunday in Lent)
Chalk Sunday

Moveable: February–April
Lent

February 14
St. Valentine's Day

Circa February 15–17
Igloo Festival

February 22
Boys' Day

February 25
St. George's Day

February 28
Feast of the Spring
Naked Festival

February 29
Leap Year Day/St. Oswald's Day

February (Full Moon)
Maka Buja

February–March (Full Moon)
Kason
Dol Purnima
Holi
Masi Magham

Pjalguna (February–March)
Sivaratri

Moon 2, Day 1 (February–March)
Wind Festival

February or March
Getting Out of the Water Festival (Ku-omboko)

Moveable: February–March (Fourteenth Day of Adar)
Purim

March

First Two Weeks in March
Festival of the Water of Youth

March 1
First of March
St. David's Day

March 3
Hina Matsuri (Girls' Day)

Circa March 5
Feast of Excited Insects

March 8
Women's Day

March 9
Feast of the Forty Martyrs

Circa Mid-March, 1 Moons after Dosmoche
Storlog

March 17
St. Patrick's Day

March 19
St. Joseph's Day
Pookhyái

Circa March 20
Ibu Afo Festival
Emume Ala

Circa March 21
Vernal Equinox

Circa March 21 and Thirteen Days Thereafter
New Year

March 25
Day of the Annunciation

Moveable: March–April (Fourth Sunday in Lent)
Mothering Sunday

Moveable: March–April (Fifth Sunday in Lent)
Carlings Sunday

March–April (Saturday before Palm Sunday)
St. Lazarus's Day (Lazarovden)

March–April (Sunday before Easter)
Palm Sunday

Moveable: March 22–April 25
Easter and Holy Week

First Sunday after Easter (Low Sunday)
Domingo de Cuasimodo
St. Thomas's Day

Day after St. Thomas's Day (Low Sunday)
Blajini Day

Second Monday and Tuesday after Easter
Hocktide

Day 25 after Easter
Feast of Rousa

Day 28 after Easter
Ropotine

Moon 3, Day 5
Pure and Bright

Moon 3, Day 23
Birthday of Matsu

March–April
Gajan of Siva
Birthday of the Monkey God
Birthday of the Lord Vardhamana
Mahavira

March–April (Full Moon)
Panguni Uttiram

Day 9, Bright Fortnight, Chaitra (March–April)
Ramanavami

March–May
Flying Fish Ceremony

April

Circa April
Road Building Festival

April
Awuru Odo
Cherry Blossom Festival
New Year

April 1
April Fools' Day

April 2
13 Farvardin/Sizdeh Bedar

April 4
St. Isidore's Day

April 5 or 6 (105 Days after the Winter Solstice)
Pure Brightness Festival

Circa April (Eight Days Beginning on Day 15 of Nisan)
Pesach/Passover

Last Day of Passover and Day after Passover
Maimona

April 12 or 13
New Year

April 13–15
New Year

April 19–25 (The Thursday in This Period)
First Day of Summer

April 23
St. George's Day

April 25
St. Mark's Day

April 30
May Eve
Walpurgis Night

Moon 4, Day 8
Buddha's Birthday

April (Various Dates)
Planting Festivals
Wangkang Festival

April–May
First of Baisakh/Vaisakh

Full Moon (Purnima) of Vaisakha (April–May)
Buddha Jayanti

May

Circa May (Day 33 of the Omer Period)
Lag Ba-omer

May
Nongkrem Dance

May (Throughout the Month)
Flowers of May

First Sunday in May
Sunday School Day

First Tuesday in May
Fool's Fair

May 1
May Day
St. Joseph's Day

May 1–May 30
Birth of the Buffalo God

May 3
Day of the Holy Cross

May 5
Cinco de Mayo

May 5 (Formerly Moon 5, Day 5)
Boys' Day

Easter to July
Holy Ghost Season

Monday, Tuesday, and Wednesday before Ascension
Rogation Days

Moveable: Forty Days after Easter
Ascension Day

Moveable: Fifty Days after Easter
Whitsun/Pentecost

First Sunday after Whitsunday
Trinity

Moveable: Thursday after Trinity
Corpus Christi/Body of Christ

Seventh Thursday after Easter
Semik

First Thursday after Corpus Christi
Lajkonik

May 11–14
Ice Saints

May 14
Crossmas

May 15
St. Sofia's Day
St. Isidore's Day

May 17
Death of the Ground

May 24
Queen's Bithday (Victoria Day)

May 24–25
Pilgrimage of Sainte Sara

May 25
St. Urban's Day

May 29
Oak-Apple Day (Royal Oak Day)

May 31
Memorial Day (Day of the Dead)

May (Full Moon)
Wesak Day

Moon 5, Day 5 (May–June)
Double Fifth
Tano

Moon 5, Day 14
Gods of the Sea Festival (and Boat Race Day)

Moon 5, Day 15
Gogatsumatsuri

May–June
Sithinakha/Kumar Sasthi
Vata Savitri
Rocket Festival

May–June (Jaistha)
Ganga Dussehra

May–June (Day 6 of Sivan)
Shavuot

May to July (Height of Rainy Season)
Okere Juju

Circa May–July
Days 1–10 of Muharram

Late May or Early June
Star Snow (Qoyllur Rit'i)

June

Early June
Tyas Tuyï

June
Egungun Festival

June 1–2
Gawai Dayak

June 11
Cataclysmos Day

June 13
St. Anthony's Day

June 13–29
Festas Juninas

June 22–August 21
Aobao Gathering

June 24
St. John's Day/Midsumer Day
Day of the Indian

June 25
Festival of the Plow

June 27–July 27
Lesser New Year

June 29
Day of St. Peter and St. Paul

June or July (Rainy Season)
Car Festival (Rath Jatra)

Moon 8, Waning Day–Moon 11, Full Moon (June/July to September/October)
Vossa/Khao Vatsa/Waso

Moon 6, Day 6
Airing the Classics

Moon 6, Day 15
Shampoo Day (Yoodoonal)

Moon 6, Day 24
Birthday of the Lotus
Yi (China) New Year

May to October, Peaking in July
Festa Season

June–July or August–September
Pola and Hadaga

Late June to Early September
Powwow

July

Circa July
Olojo Festival (Ogun Festival)

Early July
Festival of the Ears of Grain

July
Nazareth Baptist Church Festival

July 1–2
Canada Day/Dominion Day

July 2 and August 16
Palio

July 4
Independence Day/Fourth of July

July 6
Feast of San Fermin

July 8
Feast of St. Elizabeth

July 11
Naadam Festival

July 14
Bastille Day

July 15
St. Swithin's Day
Festival of the Virgin of Carmen

July 25
St. James's Day

July 26
St. Anne's Day
Pardon of Ste. Ann d'Auray

July 29
St. Olaf's Wake

Moon 7, Day 7 (July–August)
Birthday of the Seven Old Maids
Star Festival/Double Seventh

Moon 7, Days 13–15 (July–August)
Obon

Moon 7, Day 15 (July–August)
Hungry Ghost Festival

July–August
Procession of Sacred Cows
Ghanta Karna
Kandy Esala Perahera
Marya
Snake Festival
Teej
Tish-Ah Be-Av

July–August (Full Moon)
Sacred Thread Festival

July or August
Maggomboh
Imechi Festival

Late July–First Tuesday of August
Carnival

Late July or Early August
Carnival

Full Moon in Summer
Tea Meetings

August

Early August
Llama Festival

August
Good Year Festival
Panchadaan

August 1
Feast of the Progress of the Precious
    and Vivifying Cross
Honey Day
Lammas
Lúghnasa
Parents Day

August 2
Feast Day of Our Lady of the Angeles

August 2–7
Nebuta Festival

August 6
Transfiguration of Christ

August 10
Festival of St. Laurence

August 10–12
Puck's Fair

August 15
Assumption of the Virgin

August 20
St. Stephen's Fete

Circa August 24
Thanksgiving

August 30
La Rose

End of August
Reed Dance

August–September
Prachum Ben
Feast of the Dead
Festival of the Elephant God
Gokarna Aunsi

Plough Festival
Janmashtami
Lord Krishna's Birthday
Khordad-Sal
Paryushana
Agwunsi Festival
Insect-Hearing Festival

Moon 8, Day 15 (August–September)
Mid-Autumn Feast

Moon 8, Day 16 (August–September)
Birthday of the Monkey God

Various Dates
Harvest Festivals

September

Circa September
Okpesi Festival

September
Indra Jatra

September 8
Nativity of the Virgin

First and Second Days of Tishri (September–October)
Rosh Hashana

September 11
Coptic New Year
Enkutatash (New Year)

September 14
Holy Cross Day

September 15
Keiro no Hi (Respect for the Elderly Day)

Tenth Day of Tishri
Yom Kippur

12 Rabi-ul Awal (August–October)
Ma-ulid

Circa September 21–22
Autumnal Equinox
Jūgowa

September 27
Maskal

September 29
St. Michael's Day

Fifth Day of the Fifth Lunar Month (Late September–Early October)
Bon Kate

Moon 9, Day 9 (September–October)
Double Ninth
Chrysanthemum Day
Festival of the Nine Imperial Gods

Month 10 (September–October)
Ho Khao Slak

Days 24 and 25 of Tishri (September–October)
Simhat Torah and Is'ru Chag

September–October
Durga Puja/Dasain/Dussehra/Durgotsava
Oktoberfest
Pitra Visarjana Amavasya

October

Circa October (Wagyut Moon, Day 15)
Ok Pansa/Ok Vatsa/Thadingyut

October
Lord of the Earthquake

First Sunday in October
St. Michael's Day
Water Festival

Second Sunday in October
Lotu-A-Tamaiti

October 5
Han'gul Day

October 7
Festival of the Virgin of Rosario

October 17
Romería of Our Lady of Valme

October 18
St. Luke's Day

October 21
Festival of the Black Christ

October 25
St. Crispin and St. Crispinian's Day

October 26
St. Demetrius's Day

October 28
Thanksgiving
Punkie Night

October 31
All Hallow's Eve/All Saints' Eve

Moon 10, Day 1 (October–November)
Sending the Winter Dress

Moon 10, Day 25 (October–November)
Sang-joe

Kartik (October–November)
Gopashtami ("Cow Eighth") and
Govardhan Puja

October–November
Diwali/Deepavali/Tihar
Karwachoth

Seven Days, Beginning Fifteenth of Tishri (October–November)
Sukkot

Moveable: October or Later (after Rainy Season)
Mother's Day

November

Late Autumn
Keretkun Festival

Circa November
Seal Festival
Loi Krathong

Early November (Near End of Rainy Season)
Sango Festival

November
Tori-no-inchi

November 1
All Saints' Day

November 2
All Souls' Day

Friday before November 3
Creole Day

November 3
St. Hubert's Day

November 5
Guy Fawkes Night

Twenty-seventh Day of Rajab (November 6 in 1999)
Night of the Ascension

November 8
St. Michael's Day

November 11
St. Martin's Day
St. Mennas's Day

November 15
Shichi-go-san (Seven-Five-Three)

Circa November 15
Haile Selassie's Coronation Day

November 18
Feast of St. Plato the Martyr

November 19
Settlement Day

November 21
Presentation of the Virgin Mary in the
Temple

November 25
St. Catherine's Day

Fourth Thursday in November
Thanksgiving

November 30
St. Andrew's Day

Moon 8, Day 29 (November)
Seged

Month 12 (November)
Boun Phan Vet

Moveable: Month of Shaban
Shaban

Moveable: November–December
Ramadan (Month of Fasting)

December

Circa December (Tasaungmon Full Moon)
Tawadeintha/Tazaungdaing

Sunday before Advent (Early December)
Stir-Up Sunday

Four Weeks before Christmas, Beginning on a Sunday
Advent Season

Early December (Variable)
Bear Festival

Circa December (Eight Days Beginning on 25 Kislev)
Hanukkah

December 4
St. Barbara's Day

December 6
St. Nicholas's Day

December 7
Burning the Devil

Circa December 7–8
Itul

December 8
Immaculate Conception
Needle Day

Second Sunday before Christmas
Mother's Day

December 12
Our Lady of Guadalupe

December 13
St. Lucy's Day

December 14
St. Spiridion Day

December 16
Braaiveleis

December 16–25
Cock Crow Mass

Sunday before Christmas
Father's Day

Friday before Christmas
Cuci Negeri

December 18
St. Modesto's Day

Circa December 21
Ysyakh

December 21
St. Thomas's Day

Circa December 22
Winter Solstice

December 23
Festival of St. Naum
St. Thorlak's Day
La Noche de Rabanos (Night of the Radishes)

December 25–30 (Variable)
Kushi Festival

December 25
Christmas

December 26
Boxing Day
Kwanzaa
St. Stephen's Day

December 27
St. John's Day

December 28
Holy Innocents' Day

December 31
New Year's Eve
Sylvester Day

Late December
Sing-Sing

Moon 12, Day 8 (December–January)
Rice Cake Festival

Moon 12, Day 20 (December–January)
Day for Sweeping Floors

Moon 12, Day 23 or 24 (December–January)
Kitchen God Visits Heaven

Moon 12, Day 28 (December–January)
King's New Year

December–January
Little Feast

December–August
Odo

Words to Know

A

Absolute monarchy: A form of government in which a king or queen has absolute control over the people, who have no voice in their government.

Act of merit: An act of charity that, in Buddhism, is said to help the doer find favor with Buddha and earn credits toward a good rebirth.

Advent: A Christian holiday. From the Latin *adventus*, "coming," referring to the birth of Jesus. Advent is a four-week period of preparation for Christmas, beginning on the Sunday nearest November 30.

Age of Enlightenment: A philosophical movement during the eighteenth century when European writers, journalists, and philosophers influenced thousands through new ideas about an individual's right to determine his or her own destiny in life, including having a voice in government. The movement emphasized the use of reason to challenge previously accepted church teachings and traditions and thus is sometimes referred to as the Age of Reason.

Aliyah: From the Hebrew for "ascent" or "going up." The waves of Jewish immigrants to Israel in the nineteenth and twentieth centuries.

Allah: The "one God" of Islam.

Ancestors: A person's, tribe's, or cultural group's forefathers or recently deceased relatives.

Asceticism: A way of life marked by severe self-denial as a form of personal and spiritual discipline; for example, depriving the body of food and owning few material goods.

Ash Wednesday: A Christian holiday. Ash Wednesday is the seventh Wednesday before Easter and the first day of Lent, a season of fasting commemorating Jesus Christ's forty days of temptation in the wilderness. The name is derived from the practice of priests placing ashes on the foreheads of worshipers as a remembrance "that you are dust and unto dust you shall return."

B

Bastille: A castle and fortress in Paris, France, built in 1370 and later used as a prison. Bastille Day commemorates the storming of the Bastille by French peasants and workers on July 14, 1789, sparking the French Revolution.

Bee: A large gathering, usually of farm families, to complete a task and celebrate with food and drink, games, and dancing.

Beignet: A square fritter without a hole that is a popular snack during Carnival in France and French-influenced New Orleans, Louisiana. Fried pastries are popular throughout the world during Carnival, a time when people traditionally tried to use up their butter and animal fat before the Christian holiday of Lent.

Black Madonna: Poland's most famous religious icon, a painting of the Virgin Mary holding the infant Jesus, said to have been painted by Saint Luke during the first century A.D.

Blessing baskets: Baskets of Easter foods and pysanky (Easter eggs), covered with hand-embroidered cloths and carried to church to be blessed on Holy Saturday in Ukraine and Poland.

Bodhi tree: The "tree of wisdom." Buddha achieved enlightenment while sitting under a bodhi tree.

Bourgeoisie: In French, the middle social class.

Buddha: Prince Siddhartha Gautama (c. 563–c. 483 B.C.) of India, later given the name Buddha ("the Enlightened One"). His teachings became the foundation of Buddhism.

Buddhism: One of the major religions of Asia and one of the five largest religious systems in the world. Buddhists believe that suffering is an inescapable part of life and that peace can be achieved only by practicing charity, temperance, justice, honesty, and truth. They also believe in a continual cycle of birth, illness, death, and rebirth.

Byzantine Empire: The Eastern Roman Empire, with its capital at Constantinople (present-day Istanbul, Turkey).

C

Cajun: The name given to French Canadians who emigrated from Acadia, a former name for Nova Scotia. The name was eventually shortened from "Acadian" to "Cajun."

Calligraphy: Ornamental handwriting. In Islam, it is the Arabic script in which the Koran is written and which is used inside mosques as an art form.

Calypso: A popular musical style originating in Trinidad and Tobago in which singers create witty lyrics to a particular rhythm.

Carnavalesco: An individual who helps design, plan, and choreograph Carnival parades and shows in Brazil.

Caste system: A social system in which people are divided into classes according to their skin color and ancestry.

Catholic Church: The ancient undivided Christian church or a church claiming historical continuity from it.

Celts: A people who lived in Ireland, Scotland, England, Wales, and northern France before the birth of Christ, more than two thousand years ago. Also refers to modern people of these areas.

Chinese zodiac: A zodiac system based on a twelve-year cycle, with each year named after one of twelve animals. A person's zodiac sign is the animal representing the year in which he or she was born.

Christian Protestantism: Christian church denominations that reject certain aspects of Catholicism and Orthodox Christianity and believe in salvation by faith alone, the Holy Bible as the only source of God's revealed truth, and the "priesthood" of all believers.

Civil disobedience: Nonviolent action, such as protest marches, taken by an individual or group in an attempt to bring about social change.

Civil rights: Rights granted to every member of a society regardless of race, sex, age, creed, or religious beliefs. Specifically, the rights given by certain amendments to the U.S. Constitution.

Collective farm: A large farm, especially in former communist countries, formed by combining many small farms for joint operation under government control.

Colonial rule: A country's rule of a foreign land that has settlers from the ruling country, or colonists, living there.

Commedia dell'arte: Italian comedy of the sixteenth to eighteenth centuries that created some of the most famous characters in Italian costume. Among them are Harlequin, with his multicolored suit, and Punchinello, who later became a famous character in puppet shows.

Communism: A political and economic system in which the government controls and owns the means of production of goods and distributes the goods equally among the population.

Concentration camps: Nazi German military camps where civilians, primarily Jews, were held during World War II (1939–45). Millions were tortured, gassed, or burned to death in these camps.

Constitutional monarchy: A form of government in which a nation is ruled by a king or queen but the people are represented through executive, legislative, and judicial branches.

Continental Congress: Men representing twelve of the thirteen American colonies (all but Georgia) who formed a colonial government in 1774 in Philadelphia, Pennsylvania, and set forth the principles of the American Revolution (1775–83).

Cornucopia: A horn-shaped basket overflowing with vegetables and fruits. The cornucopia is a symbol of a bountiful harvest, often used as a Thanksgiving decoration. Also called "horn of plenty."

Council of Nicaea: In 325, a church governing body led by Roman emperor Constantine (reigned 306–37) met in the city of Nicaea (in what is now Turkey). The council formally established the Feast of Christ's Resurrection (Easter) and decreed that it should be celebrated on the Sunday following the first full moon after the spring equinox.

Coup d'état: A military takeover of an existing government.

Crazy days: In many European countries, the final days of Carnival celebrations, the wildest and most widely celebrated.

Creole: A person descended from or culturally related to early French or sometimes Spanish settlers of the U.S. Gulf Coast; they preserve a characteristic form of French speech and culture.

Crucifixion: A Roman method of execution, in which a person is nailed to a wooden cross to die.

Crusades: Religious wars of the eleventh, twelfth, and thirteenth centuries in which Christians fought to win the Holy Land from the Muslims.

D

Dedication: The setting apart of a temple or church for sacred uses with solemn rites.

Dharma: Laws of nature that were taught by Buddha. The primary symbol of Buddhism is a wheel with eight spokes, called the dharma wheel, which symbolizes life's constant cycles of change and the Eightfold Path to enlightenment.

Diaspora: The breaking up and scattering of a people from their homeland, especially the scattering of the Jewish people from Israel throughout the world.

Divination: Predicting the future through ritual; fortune-telling.

Dragon parade: A Chinese New Year parade featuring long dragon costumes manipulated by many dancers.

Dreidel: A four-sided top, each side marked with a Hebrew letter, all together representing the phrase "A great miracle happened there," referring to the Hanukkah miracle in ancient Jerusalem. The term also refers to the Hanukkah game played by Jewish children with the top.

Druids: An order of Celtic priests.

E

Easter bunny: Originally the Easter hare, called "Oschter Haws" by the Germans; a mythical rabbit who is said to bring colored eggs and candy to children on Easter Sunday.

Easter egg: An egg colored or decorated for Easter.

Easter lily: The white trumpet lily, native to Bermuda but widely cultivated in the United States. It blooms at Easter time and is known as a symbol of purity and of Christ's Resurrection.

Eastern Orthodox Church: A branch of the Christian church with many members in Eastern Europe, Western Asia, and the Mediterranean. The Eastern Orthodox Church began in the Greek city of Constantinople (now Istanbul, Turkey), the seat of

Roman emperor Constantine's (reigned 306–37) Eastern Roman Empire.

Elders: Older family or community members, such as grandparents, who are honored and respected for their experience and wisdom.

Enlightenment: Understanding the truth about human existence; a spiritual state marked by the absence of desire or suffering, upon which Buddhist teaching is based.

Epiphany of Our Lord: A Christian holiday. Traditionally observed on January 6, Epiphany marks the official end of the Christmas season. In Western Christian churches, Epiphany commemorates the visit of the Three Wise Men to see the infant Jesus in Bethlehem; in Eastern Orthodox churches, it is celebrated as the day of Jesus' baptism.

Epitaphion: A carved structure covered with a gold-embroidered cloth and decorated with flowers that is a symbol of Christ's tomb in the Greek Orthodox Church.

Epitaphios: "Feast of Sorrow." A Good Friday ritual in the Greek Orthodox Church, enacted as a funeral procession for Jesus Christ.

Equinox: The first day of spring and the first day of fall of each year, when the length of the day's sunlight is equal to the length of the day's darkness. This occurs on about March 20 or 21 and September 22 or 23.

Essence: The "spirit" of a thing, such as food or burnt offerings, which is believed to be usable by the dead in many cultures.

F

Fantasia: "Fantasy." Brazilian name for Carnival costume.

Fast: To voluntarily go without food or drink, often as part of religious practice, as during Ramadan or Lent.

Feudal system: The predominant economic and social structure in Europe from about the ninth to the fifteenth centuries, in which peasants farmed land for nobles and in turn received a small house and plot of land for themselves.

First fruits: The first harvesting of a crop, considered sacred by many cultures.

Folk holiday: A nonreligious holiday that originates with the common people.

Fool societies: In Germany and other parts of Europe, guilds formed by tradesmen to plan and organize Carnival celebrations.

Four Noble Truths: The four principles that became the core of Buddha's teaching: 1) Suffering is everywhere; 2) The cause of suffering is the attempt to satisfy selfish desires; 3) Suffering can be stopped by overcoming selfish desires; and 4) The way to end craving and suffering is to follow the Eightfold Path, eight steps concerning the right way to think and conduct oneself.

Freedom of the press: The right of people to publish and distribute pamphlets, newspapers, and journals containing their own thoughts and observations without censorship by government or church.

French Quarter: A historical section of New Orleans, Louisiana, where the wildest and most elaborate Mardi Gras celebrations are staged.

G

Gelt: The traditional Jewish name for money given to the poor during Hanukkah. Also refers to any Hanukkah gift and to play money (chocolate coins wrapped in gold foil) used in playing dreidel.

Gilles: A special men's society in Belgium whose members dress in identical costumes and masks and march in Mardi Gras parades.

Golden Stool of the Ashanti: A wooden stool covered with a layer of gold. The stool is sacred to the Ashanti people of Ghana, to whom it is a symbol of their nation and their king.

Good Friday: The Friday before Easter Sunday, a day for mourning Christ's death.

Gregorian calendar: The calendar in general use in much of the world in modern times. It was introduced by Pope Gregory XIII in 1582 as a modification of the Roman Julian calendar.

Griot: A storyteller who passes on the history of a people orally and through music.

Guerrilla: A member of a small military organization that uses unconventional fighting tactics to surprise and ambush their enemies.

Guillotine: A machine for beheading criminals, widely used by French revolutionaries during the late 1700s and for many years afterward in France. It consisted of a wooden frame with a heavy, tapered blade hoisted to the top and then dropped, immediately severing the victim's head.

Guising: An old Scottish custom of dressing in disguise and going from house to house asking for treats; a forerunner of Halloween trick-or-treating.

H

Hanukkiah: A Hanukkah menorah, or candleholder. It has eight main branches and a ninth for the servant candle, used to light the other eight.

Harvest festival: A festival for celebrating the gathering of crops at the end of the growing season.

Harvest moon: The full moon nearest to the time of the fall equinox (about September 23), so called because it occurs at the traditional time of harvest in the Northern Hemisphere. It appears larger and brighter than the usual full moon, and the moon is full for an extra night, giving farmers more hours to harvest crops.

Hegira: The flight of Muhammad and his followers in 622 from Mecca to Yathrib, later known as Medina, where Muhammad was accepted as a prophet. The Hegira marks the beginning of the Islamic calendar.

Hidalgo's bell: A cathedral bell rung by Father Miguel Hidalgo y Costilla in the town of Dolores on September 16, 1810, to call the native people of Mexico together in a revolt against Spanish rule.

Hinduism: The major religion of India and one of the world's oldest religions. It is based on the natural laws of dharma and conforming to one's duty through ritual, social observances, and meditation.

Holocaust: The mass slaughter by the Nazis of some six million Jews and thousands of other European civilians during World War II (1939–45), chiefly by gassing and burning the victims.

Holy Communion: A church rite in which Christians eat and drink blessed bread and wine as memorials of Christ's death. Christ is said to have initiated the rite during the Last Supper.

Holy Grail: A cup or plate that, according to medieval legend, Jesus used at the Last Supper.

Holy Land: Palestine, where Jesus Christ lived, preached, died, and was resurrected, according to the Bible. Major holy sites are Jerusalem and Bethlehem.

Holy Shroud: In the Orthodox Church in Ukraine, a specially woven and embroidered cloth that represents Jesus' burial cloth, used for Holy Week services.

I

Icons: Religious scenes or figures such as Christ and the Virgin Mary, usually very old, painted on wooden panels or on linen or cotton cloth glued to panels. Revered by Christians in the Eastern Orthodox and Catholic Churches, some are believed to have miraculous powers.

Iftar: The nighttime feast served after sunset during Ramadan.

Imam: Person who leads prayer and recites from the Koran during worship services in a mosque.

Immigrants: People who leave their home country and enter another to settle.

Islam: The major religion of the Middle East, northern Africa, parts of Southeast Asia, and some former Soviet Union countries. Islam is the world's second-largest religion. Believers, called Muslims, worship their one god, Allah, and assert that Muhammad (c. 570–632), founder of Islam, is his prophet.

Islamic calendar: The lunar calendar used to determine the date of Islamic holidays. Each of twelve months begins with the first sighting of the new moon. Each lunar month has either twenty-nine or thirty days, and each year has 354 days.

J

Jataka Tales: A collection of more than five-hundred tales said to have been told by Buddha. The tales were passed down orally through generations and finally written down several hundred years after his death. About Buddha's previous lives, the tales concern such issues as responsibility, friendship, honesty, ecology, and respect for elders.

Jesus Christ: The founder of Christianity. Jesus was born in Bethlehem in about 6 B.C. and died in about A.D. 30, when he was crucified. According to Christian tradition,

Jesus was the Son of God, and he came into the world to die for the sins of mankind. His followers believe that as Christ rose from the dead and ascended into heaven, so too will they.

Julian calendar: The calendar introduced in Rome in 46 B.C. and on which the modern-day Gregorian calendar is based.

K

Kitchen God: A Chinese deity honored during the lunar New Year. He is said to reside in the kitchen and report to the Jade Emperor (the highest deity, who resides in heaven) once a year on the actions of each household.

Koran: The Islamic holy book, written in Arabic and containing Scriptures also found in the Jewish Torah and the Christian Bible, as well as rules on all aspects of human living. The Koran is believed to have been revealed to the prophet Muhammad by Allah through the angel Gabriel.

Krewes: Secretive, members-only clubs that organize Mardi Gras parades and activities in New Orleans, Louisiana.

L

Lakshmi: The Hindu goddess of wealth, honored during Diwali, the Hindu New Year.

Last Supper: Also called the Lord's Supper; the last meal Jesus Christ shared with his disciples, believed to have been a Passover meal and at which Christ is said to have initiated the rite of Holy Communion. Christians observe the Thursday before Easter in memory of the Last Supper.

Legal holiday: A day declared an official holiday by a government, meaning that government offices, schools, and usually banks and other offices are closed so that workers may observe the holiday.

Lent: A Christian holiday. Lent is the traditional six-week period of partial fasting that precedes Easter. It is a time to remember the forty days that Jesus wandered in the desert without food. Many Christians give up a favorite food or activity during Lent.

Lunar New Year: A movable holiday marking the first day of the first lunar month on the Chinese lunar calendar. It begins at sunset on the day of the second new moon following the winter solstice (between late January and the end of February) and ends on the fifteenth day of the first lunar month.

M

Mardi Gras: *See* Shrove Tuesday.

Martyr: One who voluntarily suffers death for proclaiming his or her religious beliefs and refusing to give them up.

Masked ball: A formal dance at which those attending wear costumes and masks that conceal their identity.

Mass: A celebration of the Christian sacrament of the Eucharist (Holy Communion), commemorating the sacrifice of the body and blood of Christ, symbolized by conse-crated bread and wine.

Maundy Thursday: The Thursday before Easter Sunday, said to be the day Christ took the Last Supper, prayed in the Garden of Gethsemane, was betrayed by Judas Iscariot, and was arrested. In many church-es, this is a day for taking Holy Commu-nion in memory of the Last Supper.

Mecca: The holiest city of Islam. It is locat-ed in Saudi Arabia and is the birthplace of the prophet Muhammad. Muslims strive to make a pilgrimage to Mecca at least once during their lifetime and face toward Mecca each time they pray.

Menorah: A seven-pronged candleholder used in Jewish worship ceremonies.

Messiah: The "anointed," the Savior proph-esied in the Bible to save the world from sin. To Christians, the Messiah is Jesus Christ.

Metta: One of Buddha's main teachings, involving the concept of loving kindness. Metta is a way to overcome anger through love, evil through good, and untruth through truth.

Middle Path: A major tenant of Buddhism advocating equilibrium (balance) between extremes in life and avoiding things or ideas produced by selfish desires. Buddhists believe the best way to travel the Middle Path is through meditation, as Buddha did.

Mishnah: The Jewish code of law, passed down orally for centuries before being writ-ten down by rabbis during the second cen-tury.

Missionaries: People sent to other countries to teach their religious beliefs to native peo-ples and carry on humanitarian work.

Monk: A man who is a member of a reli-gious order and usually lives in a monastery or wanders from place to place teaching religious principles.

Monsoon: The name give to a season of heavy rains and wind in India and south-ern Asia.

Mosque: An Islamic temple for prayer and worship, consisting of a large dome and at least one pointed tower, or minaret. Mosques are decorated with calligraphy from the Koran.

Movable holiday: A holiday that falls at a different time each year, depending on the calendar used to determine the celebration. For example, Thanksgiving, Ramadan, and Easter.

Muhammad: Islam's greatest prophet. Muhammad was an Arabian who lived dur-ing the sixth century (c. 570–632). He is considered the founder of Islam.

Mumming: Merrymaking in disguise during festivals.

Muslim: A follower of the Islamic faith.

N

Nativity: The birth of Jesus Christ, as told in the biblical New Testament.

Nazarenos: Honorable men who lead Holy Week processions in Spain, wearing long robes and pointed hoods that cover their faces.

New moon: The thin crescent moon that appears after sunset following nights during the beginning of the new moon phase, when no moon can be seen. The new moon is used to mark the beginning of each month in both the Islamic and Jewish calendars.

Night of Power: The twenty-seventh night of Ramadan, which Muslims believe is the night when the angel Gabriel first began giving the words of the Koran to the prophet Muhammad.

Nirvana: A state of perfect peace and joy; freedom from greed, anger, and sorrow.

Nun: A woman who is a member of a religious order.

O

Ofrenda: Spanish word for an offering made to the dead or to a religious figure.

Oratorio: A long choral music piece for many voices, without action or scenery, usually on a religious theme. For example, Handel's *Messiah.*

P

Pagan: Referring to the worship of many gods, especially to early peoples who worshiped gods of nature.

Palm Sunday: The Sunday before Easter, when Jesus' entry into Jerusalem is com-memorated with palms, which were used to line his path.

Papier-mâché: A mixture of flour, paper, paste, and water that hardens when dry and is often used to create figures and objects for Carnival parade floats and for many other craft projects.

Parade float: A large platform that is elaborately decorated and carries people and scenery representing a specific parade theme. Floats are usually mounted on a trailer and pulled through the streets by a motor vehicle. Float design and building is often considered an art.

Parol: A traditional Filipino symbol of Christmas, a star-shaped lantern made from bamboo and paper, called the Star of Bethlehem.

Paschal candle: A large candle, sometimes weighing hundreds of pounds, that is lit in some churches on Holy Saturday and used to light many individual candles for congregation members. The Paschal candle represents Christ as the light of the world.

Passion of Jesus Christ: The sufferings that Christ endured between the night of the Last Supper with his disciples and his death by crucifixion, often reenacted by Christians during Holy Week.

Passion play: A dramatic musical play reenacting Christ's Passion and crucifixion.

Passover: An observance of the Jews' deliverance from slavery in Egypt, as told in the Bible. Jewish families were commanded to smear the blood of a sacrificial lamb on their doorways so that the angel of death would pass over their homes. Passover is still a major Jewish observance. Christians also commemorate Passover by taking Holy Communion on Maundy Thursday, the day Christ is said to have eaten a Passover meal with his disciples at the Last Supper.

Patron saint: A saint believed to represent and protect a group of people, church, nation, city or town, animals, or objects. A saint to whom people pray for help in certain circumstances.

Penitents: In Holy Week processions in Spain, the Philippines, and Central and South America, persons who walk in the procession carrying heavy wooden crosses, in chains, or whipping themselves as punishment and repentance for wrongs they have done and to commemorate Christ's suffering as he carried the Cross.

Pilgrimage: A journey, usually to a holy place or shrine.

Pilgrims: Name given to English colonists who arrived at what is now Plymouth, Massachusetts, in 1621 and settled there. This group is credited with celebrating the first Thanksgiving, with members of the Wampanoag Indian tribe.

Pongol: A sweet, boiled rice dish that is prepared to celebrate the rice harvest in parts of India. Pongol is also the name given to this holiday.

Pope: A high-ranking bishop who is head of the Roman Catholic Church and resides in the Vatican in Rome.

Proclamation: An official formal public announcement, usually by a government leader or representative.

Promised Land: According to the biblical book of Genesis, the land of Canaan, promised by God to Abraham, the father of the Jews. The prophet Moses led the Hebrews to the Promised Land after freeing them from slavery in Egypt. Refers to modern-day Israel.

Prophet: One who speaks for God or a deity; a divinely inspired speaker, interpreter, or spokesperson who passes on to the people things revealed to him or her by God.

Proverb: A wise saying or adage, often part of the cultural heritage of a people.

Puritans: Members of a sixteenth- and seventeenth-century religious Protestant group in England and New England that believed in a strict work ethic and opposed ceremony and celebration.

Pysanky: Ukrainian and Polish Easter eggs created by using the wax resist, or batik, method.

R

Rabbi: A Jewish religious teacher and leader.

Reincarnation: A Hindu belief that all life is part of a universal creative force called Brahman and that human and animal souls are reborn into new bodies many times before they return to Brahman.

Resurrection of Jesus Christ: The rising from the dead of Jesus Christ, the central figure of Christianity, worshiped as the son of God. The Resurrection is celebrated at Easter. Christians believe that Christ died to reconcile humans with God and that believers will have eternal life of the spirit.

S

Sabzeh: A dish of sprouts grown by Iranian families in preparation for Nouruz, the New Year celebration. The sprouts are said to absorb bad luck from the past year.

Saint: A person, usually deceased, who has been officially recognized by church officials as holy because of deeds performed during his or her lifetime.

Samba: A fast dance made famous in Rio de Janeiro, Brazil, in which the feet and hips move but the upper body is kept still. The samba is performed by large groups of dancers, called samba schools, who wear elaborate matching costumes in Carnival parades.

Samhain: An annual festival of the Celts that marked the end of the fall harvest and the beginning of winter. It is said to be the forerunner of Halloween and New Year celebrations in parts of Europe.

Sangha: A Buddhist community of monks and nuns.

Secular: Nonreligious.

Seven Principles of Kwanzaa: A set of principles developed for Kwanzaa laying out rules of living for the community of people of African descent: unity, self-determination, collective work and responsibility, cooperative economics, purpose, creativity, and faith.

Shofar: An ancient Jewish traditional trumpet-like instrument made from a ram's or antelope's horn that is blown in the synagogue during Rosh Hashanah and Yom Kippur.

Shrine: A place, either natural or manmade, set aside for worship of a god or saint; a box or structure containing religious relics or images.

Shrove Tuesday: The Tuesday before Ash Wednesday, also called Fat Tuesday (Mardi Gras in French). Shrove Tuesday is the final day of Carnival and the one on which the biggest celebrations are held. Traditionally a time for confessing sins (called "being shriven") and for using up the fresh meat and animal fat, eggs, and butter in the household before the forty-day fast of Lent.

Solstice: The first day of summer and the first day of winter in the northern hemisphere, when daylight hours are the longest and shortest, respectively. The solstices fall about June 22 and December 22 of each year.

Spring couplets: Two-line rhymes written in Chinese calligraphy that are displayed during Chinese New Year as a wish for good luck.

Star of David: A six-pointed star believed to have decorated the shield of King David of Israel, who ruled about 1000 B.C. A widely used symbol of Judaism.

Stations of the Cross: The locations in Jerusalem and the corresponding events leading to the Crucifixion and Resurrection of Christ. A central theme of Christian religious art and sculpture, Holy Week processions, and Passion plays.

Steel drum: A drum created in Trinidad and Tobago, originally by using discarded steel oil barrels. Steel drum bands and music have become popular worldwide.

Suhur: The pre-dawn meal served each morning of Ramadan.

Supernatural: Transcending the laws of nature; referring to ghosts and spirits and the spiritual realm.

Superstition: A belief that something will happen or not happen as a result of performing a specific ritual, for example, eating certain foods to bring good luck.

Swahili: A major African language. Many of the terms relating to Kwanzaa are drawn from Swahili.

Synagogue: A Jewish house of worship.

T

Tableau: A group of people in costume creating a living picture or scene portraying a historical, mythological, musical, or narrative theme.

Taboo: Something forbidden by religious or cultural rules, sometimes because of the fear of punishment by supernatural powers.

Talmud: The authoritative book of Jewish tradition, consisting of the Mishnah and

the Gemara, comments of rabbis about the Mishnah.

Tamboradas: Loud, steady drumbeats that sound in many Spanish cities and villages beginning at midnight on Holy Thursday and continuing until late on Holy Saturday night, announcing the Passion and death of Christ.

Throws: Objects such as plastic bead necklaces and coins, flowers, candy, or fruit thrown to the crowd from parade floats or by marching groups, especially in Carnival parades.

Torah: The Jewish holy book, consisting of the five books of Moses (first five books of the biblical Old Testament), also called the Pentateuch.

Trick-or-treating: A widely popular Halloween tradition for children in which they dress in costumes and go from door to door collecting candy and treats. Children once played tricks on those who did not give treats.

V

Vaya: A sprig of bay or myrtle attached to a small cross made from a palm frond, given by Greek Orthodox priests to members of their congregation on Palm Sunday.

Vegetarian: Eating no meat, and sometimes no animal products, such as dairy foods or eggs.

Viceroy: The governor of a country or territory who rules in the name of a king or queen.

Virgin of Guadalupe: The Virgin Mary, mother of Jesus Christ, as she is said to have appeared (with dark skin and Mexican Indian clothing) to an Indian woodcutter in 1531. She is the patron saint of Mexico's poor.

W

Witch: A woman accused of worshiping Satan and casting spells to help him do evil to humans. Witches are often fictitious characters and the subject of Halloween costumes.

Y

Yule log: A large log burned in a fireplace during the Christmas season, a custom that began in early Europe and Scandinavia.

Z

Zakat: Money given by Muslims to help the poor in obedience to the laws of Islam and as a means of worshiping Allah.

Zion: The name of a fortification in the ancient city of Jerusalem, capital of King David's kingdom in about 1000 B.C. For centuries, Zion has been a symbol of the Promised Land (Israel) and of Judaism.

Zionism: A movement to rebuild the Jewish state in Israel; from the word Zion, another name for Jerusalem.

Zoroastrianism: The ancient religion of Persia, developed by the prophet Zoroaster (c. 628–551 B.C.). Believers perform good deeds to help the highest deity, Ahura Mazda, battle the evil spirit Ahriman.

Junior Worldmark Encyclopedia of

World Holidays

Hanukkah

Also Known As:
Chanukah
Festival of Lights
Festival of Illumination
Feast of Dedication
Feast of the Maccabees

Introduction

Hanukkah (pronounced HAH-nuh-kuh) is not considered a major Jewish holy day, but it has long been one of the most popular holidays in the Jewish year, especially among children. It is celebrated for an eight-day period in December, during which families participate in special candle-lighting ceremonies, eat traditional foods, and in more recent times, exchange gifts. Because it is not a major religious holiday, both schools and places of business are open. The word "Hanukkah" means "rededication"; the holiday is often called the Feast of Dedication.

History

References to Hanukkah in ancient religious writings reveal little information about how the festival became established in Jewish tradition. The few sources that mention Hanukkah appeared long after the holiday was first celebrated, so it is difficult to distinguish between legend and real history.

The Maccabees and the miracle in the temple

During the second century B.C., the Jews in the tiny country of Judea (in the vicinity of present-day Israel) came under the domination of the Syrian-Greek king Antiochus IV (c. 214–164 B.C.). Antiochus was a tyrant who tried to force his religion on the Jews. He desecrated the Holy Temple in Jerusalem by setting up statues of Greek gods and offering sacrifices to these gods on its main altar. He also forbade the Jews from practicing Judaism and tried to force them to worship idols, or representations of gods made from stone, gold, or other materials.

According to well-established tradition, a man named Mattathias and one of his sons, called Judah the Maccabee (pronounced MA-kuh-bee; hammer), eventually led a revolt against Antiochus and the Syrians. The small band of rebels, who came to be known as the Maccabees, declared war against a vast Syrian army of almost twenty thousand soldiers.

The Maccabees fought with sticks, stones, and farm tools fashioned into weapons. The Syrian forces were much better armed, and used elephants as tanks when going into battle. After several years of fighting, in which thousands of Syrian soldiers died, the Maccabees recaptured the

Holiday Fact Box: Hanukkah

Themes

Hanukkah commemorates the rededication of the temple in Jerusalem in 165 B.C., when a one-day supply of sacred oil miraculously burned for eight days. It also celebrates a military victory that restored religious freedom to the Jews.

Type of Holiday

Hanukkah is a Jewish holiday celebrated by all three divisions of Judaism: Conservative, Orthodox, and Reform. It is celebrated in countries throughout the world.

When Celebrated

Hanukkah is celebrated for eight days, beginning on the twenty-fifth day of the Jewish calendar month of Kislev, which usually falls in December.

capital city of Jerusalem in a great victory and the Syrian army was forced to retreat.

The Jews reclaimed the temple and set about to again make it holy. They cleansed and purified it and replaced the altar with a new one made of stone. When they finished purifying the temple and erecting the new altar, they set the twenty-fifth day of the month of Kislev (November/December) as the date for dedicating the structure. This date was exactly three years after Antiochus had defiled the temple.

To rededicate the temple, the Jews needed to rekindle the sacred lamp known as the menorah (pronounced muh-NORE-uh), a seven-pronged candleholder used in Jewish worship. They could find only one container of oil that had not been opened and defiled by the Syrians. The container held only enough oil to burn in the menorah for one day. Miraculously, however, the oil burned for eight days and nights, long enough to complete the rededication. Judah Maccabee declared that these eight days be set aside for rejoicing in all the years to follow. Hanukkah, which means "rededication," commemorates this miracle that occurred at the rededication of the Holy Temple in Jerusalem more than 2,100 years ago.

Early rules about the Hanukkah lights

Because Hanukkah was celebrated with lighting candles, it also became known as Urim, meaning "lights." The practice of lighting candles became less common with time until no one seemed to remember why the ceremony had been called the Festival of Lights to begin with. The custom of celebrating with lights had spread beyond Jerusalem, however, and eventually religious leaders made kindling the lights mandatory for every Jew.

In early celebrations of Hanukkah, in accordance with Jewish law, the lighting of the Hanukkah lamp was supposed to take place between sunset and the time the last "wayfarer" was off the street. It was to be placed outside the entrance to the house; if one lived on an upper story, it was supposed to be placed on the windowsill closest to the street. If there was danger of religious persecution, the lamp could be placed on an interior table.

Medieval Hanukkah customs

In the Middle Ages (about A.D. 500–1500), Hanukkah became a very popular festival. Most Jews burned Hanukkah lamps. Women in some areas did not work while the lights were burning and sometimes did not work during the entire eight days. It was during this time that feasting at Hanukkah became a custom. One food that became especially popular was *latkes* (pronounced LOT-kuhz), or pancakes.

The Middle Ages produced the hymn that became a standard for eastern European Jews, "Maoz Tzur." Also called "Rock of Ages," it was composed by thirteenth-century poet Mordecai Ben Isaac. The hymn was sung after the Hanukkah lights were kindled. Card playing, which was discouraged by some religious leaders, also became a traditional form of celebration near the end of the Middle Ages.

Modern-day Hanukkah celebrations

Children and adults still play cards at Hanukkah, but the most popular game is played with a four-sided spinning top called a *dreidel* (pronounced DRAY-duhl). In modern-day Israel, Hanukkah is marked by a torch relay race starting in the city of Modin, where the Maccabees began their revolt and where they are buried. The celebrations commemorate the triumph of a small band of Jews over a large Syrian army and the Jews' struggle for survival.

Folklore, Legends, Stories

In addition to the story of the defeat of the Syrians by the Maccabees, two

Judah the Maccabee slaying the enemy. Judah's small band of rebels declared war against a vast Syrian army and recaptured the temple in Jerusalem. Reproduced by permission of the Corbis Corporation (Bellevue).

stories about Jewish women are often told during Hanukkah. One is about Judith, whose story is part of the Book of Judith, which is included in holy writings called the Apocrypha (pronounced uh-PAH-kruh-fuh; hidden writings). The other story is about a Jewish woman and her seven sons. It is told in the Book of Maccabees, also part of the Apocrypha. The name Hannah was given to the woman by a sixteenth-century Spanish scholar.

Brave Judith and the thirsty general

Judith was an attractive Jewish woman who lived during the second century B.C. in the town of Bethulia. The town was surrounded by Assyrian soldiers under the leadership of the general Holofernes. The Assyrians had sealed off the city so that the people could not get food and had stopped the flow of water from their spring. The Jews were dying of hunger and thirst.

One day, Judith thought of a way to save her town. She dressed in her most beautiful clothes and jewelry and walked to the camp of Holofernes, where she asked to see the general, saying she had an important message for him. Judith told Holofernes that God would abandon her people when they were forced by starvation to eat meat that was forbidden by religious law. She offered to signal the Assyrians when that time came if the general would allow her to come and go as she pleased. Holofernes agreed.

Over the next four days, Judith visited Holofernes often. On the fourth night, the general invited her to a banquet in the camp. She brought a basket filled with cheese dishes and jugs of wine. Alone with the general, Judith offered him cheeses from her basket. Holofernes became thirsty from eating the cheese, and Judith poured him a large cup of wine. She continued to refill his cup until the general became drunk and fell asleep. Then Judith took his sword and cut off his head.

As the Assyrian soldiers slept, Judith quietly left the camp and returned to Bethulia, with the head of Holofernes in her basket. The Jews hung the general's head from the city gates where his soldiers could see it the next morning. They fled from Bethulia in terror, and the town was saved from attack. Judith was honored for her bravery.

Hannah and her faithful sons

One day, a Jewish woman given the name Hannah, was walking in Judea with her seven sons. At this time, the city was under the rule of Antiochus IV and his Greek-Syrian soldiers. Antiochus stopped Hannah and ordered her sons, one by one, to eat meat from a roasted pig, even though he knew their religious laws forbade them to eat pork. One by one, Hannah's sons refused to eat the meat and were put to death in front of their mother. Even the last son, only three years old, stood fast in his religious teachings and refused to obey Antiochus's command. He, too, was killed. Then Hannah herself died for her faith.

American poet Henry Wadsworth Longfellow (1807–1882) wrote about her courage in his play *Judas Maccabaeus*. In these lines, from "The Dungeon in the Citadel," Hannah tells herself,

> Be strong, my heart!
> Break not till they are dead,
> All, all my Seven Sons;
> Then burst asunder,
> And let this tortured and tormented
>   soul
> Leap and rush out
> Like water through the shards
> Of earthen vessels broken at a well.

Customs, Traditions, Ceremonies

Hanukkah is a time for celebrating and feasting. In fact, Jewish law says there should be no mourning or fasting during these eight days. The main ceremony for Hanukkah is the kindling of the Hanukkah lamp, or *hanukkiah* (pronounced hah-NOO-kee-ah). Afterward, children play games, play cards, tell stories, and sing Hanukkah

Hanukkah Celebration in a Concentration Camp

For centuries and through many times of trouble, Jewish people have held on to their faith and, when necessary, have observed their holy days in secret. One of the most desperate of these times was during World War II (1939–45), when Nazi German soldiers put to death some six million Jews and imprisoned countless others in concentration camps. This time has come to be known as the Holocaust. A rabbi (a Jewish religious leader) was imprisoned in one of the camps, and lived to tell about a Hanukkah observance during wartime. His story was retold in an article published in the *Jerusalem Post*.

The day before Hanukkah, Nazi soldiers had beaten and shot hundreds of men from the sleeping quarters where the rabbi stayed. But on the following evening, the remaining men made a *hanukkiah* (pro-nounced hah-NOO-kee-ah), a Hanukkah lamp, from a wooden shoe, using black shoe polish for oil and strings pulled from a camp uniform as a wick.

As the ill and starving men gathered around, the rabbi lit the hanukkiah and chanted the first two blessings. Then he came to the third blessing, which says, "Blessed art Thou, O Lord our God, King of the Universe, who has kept us alive, and has preserved us, and enabled us to reach this season." Because this blessing was usually said on joyous occasions, the rabbi hesitated. So many men had died the day before, and the blessing did not seem to fit. But when the rabbi saw the faces of those still living, he continued with the third blessing for the sake of the faithful who lit the Hanukkah candles in the face of death.

songs. Gift giving has also become a popular Hanukkah tradition.

The Hanukkah lights

Because lighting the Hanukkah lamp is a way to remember the miracle of the oil that burned for eight days in the temple at Jerusalem, there are special rules regarding the way the lamp is lit and how it is displayed. The hanukkiah should be lit on each night of Hanukkah, as soon as possible after sundown, and should be placed near a window so it can be seen from the outside. It should be seen from the outside because it is important to call public attention to the miracle celebrated during the holiday. The ceremony is usually performed in each Jewish home, rather than in the synagogue (pronounced SIN-uh-gog), a Jewish place of worship.

The Hanukkah candles represent the miracle in the temple, so they are not used to provide light in the room or for any other purpose. Some families, especially in Middle Eastern countries, still use eight small lamps that burn olive oil instead of candles in the hanukkiah.

Plays, Poems, and Stories About Hanukkah

Judas Maccabaeus (play, 1872) by Henry Wadsworth Longfellow

"The Feast of Lights" (poem, c. 1880) by Emma Lazarus

"Zlateh the Goat" (story, 1966) by Isaac Bashevis Singer

"The Power of Light" (story, 1980) by Isaac Bashevis Singer

"The Blessing" (story, c. 1987) by Peninnah Schram

The Christmas Menorahs (book, 1995) by Janice Cohn

Candles are placed in the lamp from right to left but are lit from left to right. None of the eight candles can be used to light the others. For this reason, a ninth candle, called the *shammash* (assistant or servant) is used to light the Hanukkah candles. Its place in the hanukkiah is always slightly above, below, or standing apart from, the other candles or lamps. The eight Hanukkah candles are placed in a straight line, all at the same level.

Each night of Hanukkah, another candle is lighted, so that by the last night, all eight candles are lit. Every member of the family should take at least one turn at lighting the Hanukkah lamp. Women are especially encouraged to play an active part in lighting the lamps, in honor of the bravery of Judith, who saved her people from the Assyrians more than two thousand

years ago (see "Folklore, Legends, Stories"). It is Jewish tradition that women do not work while the Hanukkah lamp is burning.

The Hanukkah blessings

Before lighting the Hanukkah candles, the shammash is lit and two special blessings are said:

> Blessed is the Lord our God, Ruler of the Universe, by Whose mitzvot (commandments) we are hallowed, Who commands us to kindle the Hanukkah lights.
>
> Blessed is the Lord our God, Ruler of the Universe, Who performed wondrous deeds for our ancestors in days of old, at this season.

On the first night of Hanukkah, a third blessing is also chanted. This blessing is said at the beginning of all Jewish holidays:

> Blessed is the Lord our God, Ruler of the Universe, for giving us life, for sustaining us, and for enabling us to reach this season.

After these blessings are spoken, the Hanukkah candles are lit, from left to right, using the shammash. Once the candles are lit, they should be allowed to burn for at least half an hour. The candles should not be put out but should be left to burn out on their own. Fresh candles are used to replace the candles that have burned down the previous day. On the eighth night of Hanukkah, all the candles in the hanukkiah are burning.

Once the hanukkiah is lit, family members say other blessings and read or recite from religious texts. The "Hanerot Hallalu" ("These Candles") is either recited or sung:

> These candles we kindle to recall the miracle and wonders and the battles that You carried out for our ancestors in those days and at this season through Your holy

priests. Throughout all eight days of Hanukkah, these lights are sacred; we may not use them except to look upon them to thank You and praise Your great name for Your miracles, Your wonders, and Your deliverance.

Celebrants often recite Psalm 30, called "A Song for the Dedication of the Temple," and chant the Hanukkah prayer Al Hanisim (For the Miracles). Then they sing the hymn "Maoz Tzur" ("Rock of Ages") and other Hanukkah songs. Families also pray and read the Torah (Jewish holy book) each morning and say prayers after meals.

Gelt and other gifts

The custom of giving gifts during Hanukkah began when Jewish families gave money, or *gelt,* to the poor, to schoolteachers, and then to their children and grandchildren. Today, some parents give a small gift to their children on each night of Hanukkah. Others give one big gift. Many parents and other relatives still give children money during Hanukkah. To enhance the spirit of giving, some parents encourage their children to give a toy they no longer play with to organizations that provide gifts to the poor.

Although the Christian holiday of Christmas and the Jewish Hanukkah are unrelated in religious ways, they share the secular custom of gift giving, especially in the United States.

Foods, Recipes

Latkes, or pancakes, are a favorite food during Hanukkah. Some people say that because they are fried in oil, latkes are a reminder of the single container of oil that burned for eight days in the Holy Temple in Jerusalem. Cheese pancakes are also associated with the story of Judith, who plotted to save her people by giving the Syrian general Holofernes cheese and wine (see "Folklore, Legends, Stories"). It was a

Latkes (Potato Pancakes)

Ingredients

6 large potatoes, peeled and finely grated

1 medium onion, grated

3 eggs, lightly beaten

3 tablespoons self-rising flour

1½ teaspoons salt

½ teaspoon pepper

vegetable oil for deep frying

Directions

1. Press grated potatoes and onions in paper toweling to squeeze out as much liquid as possible.

2. Stir all ingredients together in a large bowl.

3. Heat about ½ inch of oil in a large, heavy skillet.

4. Spoon two tablespoons of the potato mixture into the oil for each pancake and flatten a little with the back of the spoon. Fry until golden on both sides, turning once.

5. When done, drain latkes on paper towels to absorb some of the oil. Keep them warm in the oven until all the pancakes are ready.

6. Serve with small dishes of applesauce and sour cream.

custom for many years to eat dairy foods during Hanukkah.

When potatoes became plentiful during the Hanukkah season, people began making pancakes from shredded potatoes. Latkes can also be made from shredded carrots, cauliflower, zucchini, sweet potatoes, or apples.

Jelly doughnuts

Jelly doughnuts, or *sufganiyot* (from the Greek word *sufgan,* meaning "puffed and fried"), are another popular Hanukkah treat. They, too, are fried in oil in remembrance of the miracle of the oil in the temple at Jerusalem. These pastries are a special favorite among Jews in Israel.

Arts, Crafts, Games

The Star of David, a symbol of the Jewish faith, is often used as a decoration during Hanukkah. The Star of David, also known as Magen David (Shield of David), is the six-pointed star believed to have decorated the shield of King David, who ruled Israel about three thousand years ago. It was believed to have magical powers. The Hanukkah menorah, with its colorful candles burning brightly in a window or on a tabletop, is also a sign of the season. Children playing with the four-sided tops called dreidels—using chocolate coins wrapped in gold foil as "money"—and opening gifts wrapped in colorful paper add more festivity to the holiday.

Dreidel: The "miracle" top

A favorite game children play during Hanukkah is Spin the Dreidel. The dreidel is a small, flat-sided top that rotates on a central axis or stem. Each of the four sides bears a Hebrew letter: *nun, gimmel, hay,* or *shin.* Together, the letters stand for "A great miracle happened there," a reference to the burning of the menorah in the temple at Jerusalem for eight days on a one-day supply of oil.

To play the game Spin the Dreidel, players are each given an equal supply of gelt—chocolate coins wrapped in gold foil, raisins, nuts, or pennies. Each player puts one or more pieces into a pile, or "pot," and then takes a turn spinning the dreidel. If it lands with the letter *nun* facing up, the player takes nothing and the spin goes to the next player; if it lands with *gimmel* facing up, he or she takes everything in the pot; on *hay,* the player takes half; and on *shin* he or she adds one coin or other object to the pot. When the pot is empty, everyone puts in one more coin and plays until one player has taken all the gelt.

Older players make the game more challenging by using the points assigned to each letter; Hebrew letters have number values. Each time a player spins the dreidel, he or she receives the number of points associated with the letter facing up when it falls.

The letter *nun* has a number value of 50, so the player gets 50 points; *gimmel* has a value of 3; *hay* a value of 5; and *shin* a value of 300. The points for each of the four letters totals 358, which is the same as the number value for the Hebrew word for Messiah—Moshiach. After a set number of rounds, the player who has the most points wins. In some games, players draw a circle two feet across, and anyone who spins the dreidel outside the circle loses a turn.

Sufganiyot (Jelly Doughnuts)

Ingredients

2 packages dry yeast

3½ cups all-purpose flour

2 eggs plus 1 egg with white and yolk separated

½ cup lukewarm water

½ cup milk

⅓ cup softened butter or margarine

¼ cup sugar

1 teaspoon salt

1 teaspoon cinnamon

1 teaspoon nutmeg

your favorite jelly or jam for filling

vegetable oil for deep frying

Directions

1. Dissolve yeast in warm water in a large bowl, then heat milk until steaming.
2. Add sugar, salt, and butter or margarine to the hot milk and stir. When milk mixture feels warm to the touch, add to yeast and water in bowl.
3. Add the 2 eggs plus 1 egg yolk, spices, and 2 cups of the flour. Mix well, using an electric mixer.
4. Mix in the remaining 1½ cups of flour using a wooden spoon.
5. Turn the mixture out on a floured board and knead for 2 or 3 minutes, then place dough back into bowl and cover with a towel. Let rise for about 1 hour in a warm, draft-free place.
6. Punch down and knead for 2 more minutes on floured board, then let sit about 10 minutes.
7. Roll dough out to about ¼-inch thickness.
8. Use the rim of a drinking glass or a biscuit cutter to cut out an even number of circles of dough.
9. Put a spoonful of jelly or jam in the center of half of the circles and brush the outside of each circle with the beaten egg white.
10. Place a plain dough circle over each jelly circle and press the edges together so the egg white will seal them.
11. Place the doughnuts on a floured baking sheet and cover with a towel. Let rise about 1 more hour.
12. Heat 2 inches of oil in a large, heavy skillet and fry the doughnuts, a few at a time, turning when they rise to the surface. Both sides should be golden brown.
13. Remove and drain on paper towels. Sprinkle with granulated sugar or confectioner's sugar.

Makes about 1½ dozen jelly doughnuts

On the first night of Hanukkah a young boy prepares to light the menorah under the supervision of his sister and father at their Brooklyn, New York, home in 1995. Reproduced by permission of AP/Wide World Photos.

Symbols

The two symbols most associated with Hannukkah are the menorah and the dreidel.

Hanukkah menorah

The menorah, which has always been a part of Jewish celebrations, is the most important symbol of Hannukah. The first menorahs were small, individual clay lamps used to burn oil. Over time, candles were substituted for oil. The menorah is thought to have originated in biblical times

as a seven-branched religious symbol. According to the Torah, the artist Bezalel was told by God to create a seven-branched menorah.

The Hanukkah menorah, called the hanukkiah, is different from the original temple menorah. Instead of seven branches, it has eight. It also has a place in the middle for a ninth candle, known as the shammash, or "servant," candle. Because the original eight Hanukkah lights, representing the eight days the menorah miraculously burned in the temple in Jerusalem, were considered holy, one could not be used to kindle the others. For this reason, the shammash candle came into use as a means of lighting the other candles.

The earliest known object used as a Hanukkah lamp was discovered in a cave near Jerusalem. Carved from a piece of limestone, it contained eight slots for holding olive oil and wicks. The menorah dates from the second century B.C., about four hundred years after the first Hanukkah celebration.

Placing the Hanukkah lamp: Hanukkah lamps were originally placed outside the door opposite the mezuzah (pronounced muh-ZOO-zuh), a religious scroll kept in a special case attached to the right side of the doorpost. In times of religious persecution, however, the rabbis allowed the menorahs to be placed indoors.

Because the menorahs were no longer exposed to the weather or to theft, craftsmen began to experiment with more artistic designs. They began making more expensive candleholders made of silver and other metals fastened to a horizontal base. Later, they added a back wall both to protect the menorah from heat and so it could be hung from a nail on the doorpost or elsewhere.

Regional influences: Later menorah designs incorporated features of the country where they were made. In Spain, for example, the back wall of a menorah often resembled Moorish arches. French menorahs might feature a small replica of the Cathedral of Notre Dame, a gothic cathedral built during the Middle Ages in Paris. And in Italy, craftsmen incorporated the elaborate designs of the Renaissance period (fourteenth to sixteenth centuries) in their menorahs.

Today, most menorahs are mass-produced, although artisans still turn out a huge array of designs. Subjects range from such fanciful scenes as the biblical story of Noah's Ark to somber depictions of the Holocaust, the time during World War II when millions of Jews were put to death by Nazi German soldiers. No matter what the design, the Hanukkah menorah brings to life the story of the brave fight for religious freedom and the miracle of the one-day supply of oil that burned for eight days.

In modern-day Israel, giant electric-light menorahs adorn the top of the Knesset (parliament building) and other public buildings during Hanukkah. In the capital, Tel Aviv, all the lights are left on at night, so during Hanukkah it is called "the City of Lights."

Dreidel

A four-sided top called a dreidel is used to play a favorite Hanukkah game (see "Arts, Crafts, Games"). The dreidel is called *sevivone* in Hebrew, which means "to turn." On each of the four sides of the dreidel is one of four Hebrew letters—*nun, gimmel, hay* or *shin*. These letters are initials for the Hebrew words *Nes Gadol Hayah Sham,* which means "A great miracle happened there."

In Israel, the letter *shin* is replaced with the letter *pay,* so that the dreidel's letters stand for "A great miracle happened *here*" ("Nes Gadol Hayah Po"). The "great miracle" happened when the Jews were restoring the Holy Temple at Jerusalem and the single container of oil, enough for only one day, burned for eight days.

Dreidels were originally carved from wood, but now they are made from metal or plastic. They are always colorful, painted with the four letters and designs in bright blues, gold or white, red, and green.

An undercover game: The game of dreidel was originally a German gambling game played on Christmas Eve. It is said to have been introduced to Europe during the Middle Ages by emigrants from India. A similar game was probably played by the ancient Greeks and Romans. Legend has it that the dreidel was often used as a "cover" in places where Jews were forbidden to practice their religion. During the Greek occupation of Judea, for example, Jews would gather to study the Torah. If a Greek officer found them congregating, they would pretend to be playing with the dreidel.

Reminder of a miracle: Spin the Dreidel was originally a game in which players could win or lose money, called gelt, depending on the letter that was on top when the dreidel stopped spinning and fell over. In German, the letters *n, g, h,* and *s* stood for *nichts* (nothing), *ganz* (all), *halb* (half), and *stell ein* (put in), and told the players what to do when the top landed with one of these letters facing up. Rabbis allowed Jews

A rabbi hands out dollar bills to students before they board a school bus for the ride home in Brooklyn, New York, in 1999. The giving of a small gift, Hanukkah gelt, is part of the celebration of Hanukkah. Reproduced by permission of AP/Wide World Photos.

to play this gambling game on Hanukkah, and after a while the dreidel's four letters were given their Hebrew names and assigned the meaning "A great miracle happened there" to remind Jews of the reason they celebrated the holiday.

Music, Dance

During Hanukkah, a number of traditional songs are sung in both English and Hebrew. Some are religious songs and others are just for fun, including two songs about the dreidel: "Dreidel, Spin, Spin, Spin" and "I Have a Little Dreidel." A thirteenth-century poet named Mordecai Ben Isaac wrote the song "Maoz Tzur" ("Rock Fortress"), also known as "Rock of Ages." The English version was written by Gustav Gottheil (1827–1903) and M. Jastrow (1861–1921).

Rock of Ages, let our song
Praise Thy saving power;
Thou amidst the raging foes
Wast our shelt'ring tower.
Furious they assailed us,
But Thy arm availed us,
And Thy word
Broke their sword
When our own strength failed us.

Another song about the battle against Antiochus IV and the Syrians is "Who Can Retell," or "Mi Yemalel":

Who can retell,
the things that befell us,
Who can count them?
In every age a hero or sage,
Came to our aid.
Hark! In days of yore in Israel's
ancient land,
Brave Maccabeus led the faithful
band.
But now all Israel must as one arise,
Redeem itself through deed and
sacrifice.

The song "Hanukkah" is about modern celebrations of the holiday:

Oh Hanukkah, oh Hanukkah, come
light the Menorah,
Let's have a party; we'll all dance the
hora.
Gather round the table, we'll give you
a treat.
Sevivon to play with, latkes to eat.
And while we are playing the candles
are burning low.
One for each night, they shed a sweet
light,
To remind us of days long ago.

Special Role of Children, Young Adults

Hanukkah is a joyous holiday that includes children in every activity, from lighting the Hanukkah lamp to spinning the dreidel and helping prepare special foods, such as latkes, cookies, and doughnuts. Children also receive gifts at Hanukkah; many give gifts as well. They are included in reciting blessings, reading from the Torah, singing songs, and reading stories. Children may make Hanukkah crafts, including their own dreidel and hanukkiah.

For More Information

Berger, Gilda. *Celebrate! Stories of the Jewish Holidays*. New York: Scholastic Press, 1998.

Drucker, Malka. *The Family Treasury of Jewish Holidays*. Boston: Little, Brown, 1994.

Kimmel, Eric A., ed. *A Hanukkah Treasury*. New York: Henry Holt, 1998.

Zalben, Jane Breskin. *Beni's Family Cookbook for the Jewish Holidays*. New York: Henry Holt, 1996.

Web sites

"Celebrate Hanukkah." [Online] http://www.caryn.com/holiday/holiday-Hcelebrate.html (accessed on January 31, 2000).

"Chanukah." [Online] http://www.vjholidays.com/chanukah (accessed on January 31, 2000).

"Chanukah on the Net." [Online] http://holidays.net/chanukah (accessed on January 31, 2000).

"Hanukkah." [Online] http://www.joi.org/celebrate/hanuk (accessed on January 31, 2000).

"JewishHoliday.com: A Family Friendly Guide." [Online] http://www.jfhanukkah.com (accessed on January 31, 2000).

Hanukkah Sources

Black, Naomi. *Celebration: The Book of Jewish Festivals*. Middle Village, N.Y.: Jonathan David Publishers, 1989, pp. 56–73.

Fellner, Judith B. *In the Jewish Tradition: A Year of Food and Festivities*. New York: Michael Friedman, 1995, pp. 54–67.

Klagsbrun, Francine. *Jewish Days: A Book of Jewish Life and Culture Around the Year*. New York: Farrar, Straus, Giroux, 1996, pp. 63–69.

Raphael, Chaim. *Festival Days: A History of Jewish Celebrations*. New York: Grove Weidenfeld, 1990, pp. 89–93.

Strassfeld, Michael. *The Jewish Holidays: A Guide and Commentary*. New York: Harper & Row, 1985, pp. 161–76.

Thompson, Sue Ellen, ed. *Holiday Symbols 1998*. Detroit, Mich.: Omnigraphics, 1998, pp. 172–74.

Turner, Reuben. *Jewish Festivals*. In *Holidays and Festivals* series. Vero Beach, Fla.: Rourke Enterprises, 1987, pp. 22–25.

Web sites

"Hanukkah Songs." [Online] http://www1.sympatico.ca/Features/Hanukkah/songs.html (accessed on February 10, 2000).

Silverman, Philip. "Hanukkah in Bergen Belsen." *Jerusalem Post*. [Online] http://idt.net/~kimel19/hanuka.html (accessed on February 10, 2000).

"Women in Chanukah: The Stories of Hannah and Judith." [Online] http://www.vjholidays.com/chanukah/women.htm (accessed on February 10, 2000).

Independence Day

Also Known As:
Bastille Day (France)
Independence Day (Ghana, Mexico, United States)
Yom Ha'atzmaut (Israel)
Sixteenth of September (Mexico)
Fourth of July (United States)

Introduction

People in countries all over the world observe the anniversary of the date they gained independence. An example is Independence Day celebrated in the United States on July 4. Others observe the anniversary of a revolutionary event marking a fundamental and violent change in society, such as the storming of the Bastille in France. Such national holidays serve to remind individuals of the struggle for freedom and to help instill national pride. Celebrations vary from country to country, but citizens usually participate in parades, attend rallies, display national flags, and watch fireworks displays.

History

During the eighteenth, nineteenth, and twentieth centuries, a desire for self-government and a belief in each nation's right to determine its own destiny swept the world. People in nation after nation declared, and fought for, their independence from other countries. Revolutions rocked other nations as the common people overthrew oppressive rulership.

"Liberty, Equality, Fraternity"

The Bastille was a fortress used as a prison by the French government. The forceful taking of the Bastille on July 14, 1789, was a turning point in the attempt by the common people of France to achieve liberty, democracy, and freedom from a rulership that kept them poor and powerless. Celebrated since 1790, Bastille Day was officially proclaimed a national holiday in France in 1880. The French Declaration of the Rights of Man and of the Citizen, written in 1789, and the motto of the French Revolution, "Liberty, Equality, Fraternity," became a foundation for other democratic governments throughout the world.

Free Africa

On March 6, 1957, Ghana became the first African colonial state to win its independence from Great Britain. Within ten years after winning its own freedom, it was a leader in the Pan-African movement that brought independence to nearly all other British colonial states in Africa. Ghana was formerly called the Gold Coast, because its land was rich with gold. When it became a free nation, it was renamed for

Holiday Fact Box: Independence/ National Days

Themes

Independence and national days celebrate the gaining of freedom from foreign rule, internal revolutions, or victories in war.

Type of Holiday

Independence and national days are nonreligious, patriotic holidays that pay tribute to the nation.

When Celebrated

National holidays are celebrated on the anniversary of the date a country achieved independence, started a revolution, or won a major victory. France's Bastille Day is July 14; Ghana's independence is celebrated March 6; the reestablishment of the Jewish state is celebrated on May 14; Mexico's independence is celebrated on September 16; and the United States' independence day is July 4.

the great kingdom of Ghana, which flourished in West Africa a thousand years ago.

The Promised Land

Israel's Independence Day celebrates the reestablishment, on May 14, 1948, of a Jewish state in Israel. Most Jews had made their homes in other lands throughout the world for centuries, but a yearning to regain their homeland, also known as Zion, had been an enduring dream and expectation of each new generation of Jews. That dream became reality in 1948. That year, the modern state of Israel was formed by a decree of the United Nations, restoring the Jewish homeland, which had been lost two thousand years earlier.

The Cry of Dolores

Mexican Independence Day commemorates September 16, 1810, when Father Miguel Hidalgo y Costilla (1753–1811), a parish priest in the small town of Dolores, gave the cry that started the Mexican War of Independence (1810–21). The common people of Mexico rose up in arms to throw off Spanish rule, which had lasted some three hundred years. Mexico's fight for independence motivated other countries in Latin America to overthrow Spanish rule.

"All men are created equal"

Fourth of July festivities celebrate July 4, 1776, when representatives from the thirteen American colonies signed the Declaration of Independence, avowing the equality of mankind, declaring freedom from British rule, and establishing the United States of America. The colonists won their freedom in the American Revolution (1775–83). Fourth of July celebrations in the United States began in 1777. The U.S. Congress declared the Fourth of July a legal holiday in 1941. The Declaration of Independence has been a model for citizens of many other countries who seek the right to govern themselves.

Folklore, Legends, Stories

Struggles for independence from harsh rule and the fight to maintain cultural identity and religious freedom have given rise to inspiring legends that have become embedded in history. Some are true stories of a particular battle, of the coming of revolution, or of patriotic individuals. Others are fictional tales based on historical fact. In either case, they have become part of the literature and folklore of independence and are retold so that each new generation may remember them.

Ideas behind revolution and democracy

During the seventeenth and eighteenth centuries, a period known as the Age of Enlightenment, great philosophers and writers emerged in Europe. Their ideas about the equality of all people, basic civil rights, and the right of people to govern themselves were revolutionary, because many people still lived under colonial rule or absolute monarchy. A country that is not allowed to have its own government, but instead is ruled by a larger, more powerful country, is under colonial rule. A country that is a monarchy is one headed by a single ruler, known as a monarch. A monarch has absolute power and may choose not to allow citizens a voice in government.

Well-educated people read these remarkable ideas and shared them with their countrymen, triggering revolutions that opened the door for self-rule. Freedom of the press—the freedom to publish news so that all people might be informed—was critical to independence movements.

The French writer Jean-Jacques Rousseau (1712–1778) wrote about the equality of all men and their right to be represented in government. Voltaire (the pen name of François Marie Arouet; 1694–1778) wrote about the rights of men and freedom of speech, the press, and religion. English philosopher John Locke (1632–1704) influenced the thinking of the revolutionaries with his *Two Treatises on*

Fireworks explode over the Charles River in Cambridge, Massachusetts, with the Boston skyline in the background, July 4, 1997. Fireworks displays are a part of independence celebrations throughout the world. Reproduced by permission of AP/Wide World Photos.

Government (1690). These writers' ideas were reflected in the United States' Declaration of Independence, in France's Declaration of the Rights of Man and of the Citizen, and in the declarations of many nations that later achieved independence.

Customs, Traditions, Ceremonies

Each country has its own unique way of celebrating its heritage and com-

A Booming Way to Celebrate

Fireworks displays are a part of independence celebrations throughout the world. They were first used in China about eight hundred years ago. Most fireworks purchased today are still made in China, Taiwan, and other Far Eastern countries. Fireworks come in many sizes and shapes and are made from tubes filled with gunpowder and chemicals set to explode when a fuse is lit. Gases propel the fireworks into the air or across the ground, and the chemicals each produce a certain color when the fireworks explode. The whistling, popping, and bright colors bring to mind the gun and cannon fire of war. Fireworks can be heard and seen for a long way, so they have traditionally been used to announce a celebration.

memorating the efforts of those who helped ensure their freedom. Some customs that are universal include shooting off spectacular fireworks displays, decorating government buildings and homes with national flags, hosting patriotic parades and processions, and reenacting historic events.

Fireworks displays

France, Ghana, Israel, Mexico, and the United States have one major independence day custom in common—big nighttime fireworks displays. Fireworks explode in national colors, and thousands of people travel to major cities to watch the shows. In Paris, France, people line up along the Seine River to watch the Bastille Day fireworks. Cities and towns all over the United States include fireworks in their Fourth of July celebrations. People in Mexico watch fireworks displays from plazas where Independence Day fiestas are held. In Israel, people sit around bonfires late at night after the fireworks and evening festivities.

Flying flags and decorating in national colors

The national flag and national colors are on display for independence celebrations everywhere. National flags are flown by homeowners and from public buildings and shops. Crowds watching parades and military displays wave flags. In Ghana, a formal flag-raising ceremony is held at Kwame Nkrumah Circle, which is named for the father of Ghanaian independence. People attending street parties in Israel wave flags as they sing and dance.

Streets, circles, town squares, and plazas are decorated with ribbons, rosettes, banners, lights, and flowers in national colors. In Mexico, people drape statues of revolutionist Father Miguel Hidalgo with garlands of flowers. In Paris, a monument to the French Revolution is decorated with French flags.

Parades, processions, and military displays

Nearly every free nation celebrates the anniversary of its independence with parades and a display of military might. More than a million visitors visit Paris each year for its Bastille Day celebration. A main attraction is the formal military parade along the city's major boulevard. Fourth of July parades began in the United States

A group representing traditional Greek soldiers marches down a Boston, Massachusetts, street during the Greek Independence Day Parade, March 28, 1999. Nearly every free nation celebrates the anniversary of its independence with parades and a display of military might. Reproduced by permission of AP/Wide World Photos.

during the 1780s, soon after the new nation declared its independence from Great Britain. The parade ground at Independence Square in the capital city of Accra is the site of Ghana's largest Independence Day parade.

On Bastille Day in Paris, a spectacular air show features jet planes flying in formation, with smoke plumes in the national colors. In Ghana, some schoolchildren are chosen to participate in a Military Open Day at military bases. Ghanaians also enjoy military drills and arms displays.

Israel adds a touch of humor to its military events. A televised pageant makes fun of military life, with soldiers whining about being treated badly by their officers. But the nation also thrills the crowds with fly-bys of vintage planes from its 1948 War of Independence and modern fighter jets, parachutists, naval displays, and soldiers reenacting battles.

Speech making and reenactments
Making speeches was a Fourth of July tradition in the United States during the late 1700s and throughout the 1800s.

In cities and towns throughout France, mayors and dignitaries deliver Bastille Day speeches in the town square. In Ghana, lectures about independence and democratic government are broadcast on radio and television, and groups perform plays reenacting Ghana's independence story.

In Mexico, the highlight of Independence Day celebrations is the reenactment of the "Cry of Dolores." This was the yell given by Father Miguel Hidalgo in the town of Dolores, where the fight for Mexican independence began. Shortly before 11 P.M. on the eve of Independence Day in every central plaza in Mexico, cathedral bells ring and an official gives the yell, "Long live independence! Long live Mexico!" The crowd echoes the cry.

Picnics, rodeos, and outdoor excursions

Because many independence days fall during warm weather, picnicking and other outdoor activities are associated with this holiday. Rodeos are popular in the United States and Mexico, and soccer games draw big crowds in Ghana. Noonday picnics and late-night storytelling around a bonfire are favorite pastimes in Israel. Families in France might spend the day at a park, zoo, or museum. Many take summer vacations during this time and go camping, fishing, or boating. Other people simply rest from work and enjoy a backyard barbecue.

Festivals, fairs, and street parties

Independence day celebrations in many countries include a big street festival, with lots of music and dancing. In France, people gather for street dancing to live bands on the eve of Bastille Day. In Paris, firemen and other organizations sponsor balls and provide dinner and dance music. Street dancing to African drums is popular in Ghana, as are cultural displays about Ghana's tribal peoples. In Mexico, Independence Day fiestas include open-air markets at which foods, toys, arts, and crafts are sold. Israelis take to the streets to sing and dance all night, bopping one another on the head with plastic hammers, lighting sparklers, and spraying cans of plastic string.

Special memorial, religious, and honorary services

Each year on the Fourth of July, dozens of new American citizens take the oath of citizenship in Arlington, Virginia, a practice that began in 1915. National Honors and Awards ceremonies are held in Ghana on Independence Day. In Israel, Independence Day comes the day after Memorial Day, a day to remember those who gave their lives for independence.

Islamic mosques (pronounced MOSKS) and Christian churches in Ghana hold special Independence Day services, and a National Thanksgiving service may close the celebration with prayers of gratitude. In Israel, the world-famous International Bible Quiz for Jewish Youth is held on Independence Day as a way of keeping the Jewish faith in the foreground of the festivities.

Clothing, Costumes

Clothing in the national colors and native costumes are often worn on independence and national days. From the red, white, and blue top hat of "Uncle Sam," representing the United States, to Ghana's colorful *kente* (pronounced KEN-tay) cloth, clothing creates a national identity.

South Koreans dressed in traditional Korean costumes gather at the Topgol Park in Seoul in 1999 to celebrate the March First Independence Movement Day, which commemorates Korea's long struggle for independence from Japan. Reproduced by permission of AP/Wide World Photos.

During the French Revolution, the working men of Paris developed drab clothing in direct contrast to the colorful silks and satins and the tight knee pants worn by noblemen. Women wore plain dresses and curls close to their heads, the opposite of ladies of the nobility. French revolutionaries adopted the "red bonnet," a common, red wool cap, and the colors blue, white, and red became associated with the Revolution.

For many of Mexico's festivals, women wear a blouse and skirt outfit called the *china poblana*. Mexico's native Indians wear woven scarves or blankets in bright colors. Dancers in native Indian costume perform during festivals for Independence Day. Rodeo riders, bullfighters, and musicians wear fancy clothing decorated with silver that is reminiscent of the Spanish nobles who once ruled their country.

Foods, Recipes

Favorite ways to eat on independence and national days are to picnic outdoors, barbecue, or sample traditional foods at street festivals. In the United States, Fourth of July get-togethers often include hot dogs, hamburgers, and corn on the cob cooked on the grill. In Israel, family and friends get together for a *mangal,* or barbecue. On Bastille Day, French families love to picnic at the Champ-de-Mars in Paris, the site of the first Bastille Day celebration, held July 14, 1790.

In Ghana, a dish made with mashed yams and boiled eggs is often served on the morning of Independence Day. Mexico's national dish is *chiles en nogada.* It is made from stuffed green chili peppers floating in a white sauce, with red pomegranate seeds, displaying Mexico's national colors, green, white, and red.

Arts, Crafts, Games

The passion of revolution and the fight for freedom are often captured by the great artists of every country. The French artist Jacques-Louis David (1748–1825) painted from his own experiences as a member of France's National Convention during the Revolution. Two of his well-known subjects were the Tennis Court Oath and the death of Jean-Paul Marat, a revolutionary journalist. He also sketched Queen Marie-Antoinette as she rode in a cart bound for the guillotine.

Mexican muralist Diego Rivera (1886–1957) painted a mural of Father Miguel Hidalgo leading an army of poor Mexican fighters under the banner of the Virgin of Guadalupe. In 1876, American painter Archibald Willard (1836–1918) created *The Spirit of '76,* depicting three generations of an American family marching off to war.

Cartoons that circulated before and after revolutionary times also became famous. A cartoon often printed before the French Revolution showed a peasant carrying a nobleman and a priest on his back, representing unfair taxation of the poor. In the United States, "Uncle Sam" became a well-known cartoon character representing the U.S. government.

In celebration of independence

In Mexico and Ghana, native arts and crafts are displayed and sold during outdoor festivals on Independence Day. Festivities also include games or sports. In Mexico, people attend bullfights and rodeos. Ghanaians go to soccer, called football, games and watch or play tennis, polo, cricket, or golf. Americans may play softball, volleyball, or toss a Frisbee at Fourth of July picnics.

Symbols

The symbols associated with independence and national days serve as reminders of the historical events that led to a nation's freedom. They are immediately recognizable worldwide and are held sacred by citizens whose country they represent. Common independence day symbols include the national flag, buildings that featured prominently in revolutionary events, and cultural symbols.

Flags

The Tricolor: On July 17, 1789, after the fall of the Bastille, the newly elected mayor of Paris received King Louis XVI on a formal visit. The mayor presented the king with a blue, white, and red cockade (hat ornament) as a symbol that the people wanted to include their king in a new government. From that day forward, blue, white, and red became the colors of the Revolution, and the flag known as the Tricolor—with three vertical bands of blue, white, and red—was adopted as the official flag of France in 1794.

Flag of the Republic of Ghana: The flag of Ghana has three horizontal stripes: red at the top, yellow or gold in the middle, and green at the bottom, with a black star in the center, which gives it its name, the Black Star. The red band represents the blood of those who died during Ghana's struggle for independence; the yellow or gold stands for gold and other minerals that contribute to the nation's economy; and the green represents the dense forests that cover parts of the land. The black star stands for African freedom and independence.

The Israeli flag: The World Zionist Organization displayed a flag decorated with the Star of David at its first meeting in 1897. The group was founded to establish a homeland for Jews. The Star of David, or Magen David (Shield of David), is the six-pointed star believed to have decorated the shield of King David, who ruled Israel about three thousand years ago. It was believed to have magical powers and is found on many ancient architectural ruins. The flag, also bearing the blue and white stripes of a *tallith,* or Hebrew prayer shawl, became so popular that it was adopted by Israel as its national flag when it became a new nation in 1948.

The Mexican flag: Mexico's green, white, and red national flag was designed soon after Mexico won its freedom from Spain, in 1821. It was adopted as the official flag of Mexico in 1934. The flag's green stripe stands for independence, its white stripe for religious freedom, and its red stripe for unity. In the center of these three vertical stripes is a picture of an eagle standing on a cactus and holding a snake with its beak and talons. According to legend, the wandering Aztec Indians saw such an eagle and believed it to be a sign to build their capital on that spot. The city they built was Tenochtitlán (pronounced tay-NOK-tee-TLAHN) on the site of modern-day Mexico City.

"Old Glory": The first American flag was sewn by Betsy Ross (1752–1836), of Philadelphia and was adopted on June 14, 1777. The first flag had thirteen stripes, alternating in red and white, and thirteen white stars forming a circle on a blue field in the upper left-hand corner of the flag. The thirteen stripes and stars represented the original thirteen colonies. As new states were added to the Union, the number of stars increased. Today, a block of fifty stars on a blue background represents the fifty states.

The nickname "Old Glory" was given to the flag by William Driver, a ship captain, in 1831, when he was presented with a U.S. flag for his ship. The flag survived for many years, even through the American Civil War (1861–64). Today the U.S. flag is also known as "the Stars and Stripes" and "the Star-Spangled Banner."

The Bastille

The Bastille was a castle and fortress built in 1370 into an old wall surrounding Paris. Its stone walls were one hundred feet high and eight feet thick. Eight tall round towers supported its sides. When the old city wall crumbled, the Bastille was left standing, its high walls towering over the city streets.

During the seventeenth century, French kings began using the Bastille as a prison. Anyone could be imprisoned there, by order of the king. They received no trial and were not told the length of their sentence. Because of this, the Bastille symbolized one form of oppression of the French people by the monarchy (kings and queens).

Many people were imprisoned in the Bastille, among them the famous French writer Voltaire and the mysterious Man in the Iron Mask, an unknown prisoner who became the subject of many books and plays. Ironically, historians say most prisoners were treated well, especially when it came to food. One prisoner once held a dinner party for twenty friends in the Bastille; another had his own wine brought in. Even Voltaire praised the food he was served in the Bastille.

When the working people of Paris stormed the Bastille on July 14, 1789, their victory marked the beginning of the French Revolution (1789–99). Since 1790, July 14 has been celebrated each year as France's national day.

Soon after the storming of the Bastille, it was decided that the old fortress should be destroyed. One thousand workmen tore the building down and sold the stones and guns from the Bastille as souvenirs. Today, a monument has been erected at the famous site, and Bastille Day ceremonies and celebrations are held there.

The Golden Stool of the Ashanti

When the Ashanti (people of what is now Ghana) king Osei Tutu (pronounced OH-say too-too) came to power in the late 1600s, he and his chief priest devised a plan to unify the tribal clans. They called a meeting at the Ashanti capital for a ceremony to accept Osei Tutu's rule. When the people were assembled, the priest announced that Onyame, the god of creation, wanted the Ashanti to be united as one people to form a strong nation. As a sign, he was sending a golden stool from heaven.

According to tradition, the priest called upon the gods and the ancestors, and the Golden Stool came down from heaven in a big, black cloud, with thunder rumbling and thick white dust filling the air. The stool landed gently on Osei Tutu's knees. The priest offered a prayer of thanks to the spirits. Then he gave the stool to Osei Tutu and designated it the property of the Ashanti people. He declared it the Soul of the Ashanti Empire. As long as the stool was guarded and protected, the Ashanti nation would flourish, but if the stool was dishonored or fell into enemy hands, the nation would wither and die.

The Golden Stool is made of wood with a layer of gold covering it. Osei Tutu never sat on the stool; he set it next to him and rested his arm on it when he spoke to the people. It was not to touch the ground and was carried in processions as a sacred object.

Four golden figures that now adorn the stool are said to represent enemies of the Ashanti. Stored in a secret place, the Golden Stool always rests on its side to keep away evil spirits. A bell is attached to either side of the stool to call the ancestors of the ruling king. Today, the 300-year-old Golden Stool of the Ashanti is a symbol of unity, leadership, and independence for all of Ghana.

Zion

Zion was the name of a fortress in the ancient city of Jerusalem, in what is

A dancer cheers during a parade in Belize City in September 1999 celebrating the country's 1981 independence from Great Britain. Reproduced by permission of AP/Wide World Photos.

now Israel. When King David made Jerusalem the capital of his kingdom in about 1000 B.C., he made Zion one of its symbols. Through the centuries that followed, the word Zion symbolized "the Promised Land" and the collective Jewish hope of returning to the ancestral homeland. As such, it also symbolizes the Jewish people and the Land of Israel.

Hidalgo's Bell

On September 16, 1810, Father Miguel Hidalgo rang the bell in the church steeple in Dolores, Mexico, to call his people together and encourage them to fight for independence. Since that time, the church bell has been a symbol of Mexico's War of Independence. Cathedral bells are rung around the country on Mexican Independence Day, and the president of Mexico rings a replica of Hidalgo's bell on the night of September 15 to commemorate the Cry of Dolores. Many other cities and towns throughout Mexico also have a replica of Hidalgo's bell.

Liberty Bell

The famous bell that has become a symbol of freedom in the United States was made in England in 1752 for Pennsylvania's fiftieth anniversary celebration. Inscribed on the bell are words from the biblical book of Leviticus: "Proclaim Liberty throughout all the land unto all the inhabitants thereof." The Liberty Bell is pictured on the back of U.S. half-dollars.

Music, Dance

The national anthem of each country is the most representative song for independence and national days. The United States' "Star-Spangled Banner," Israel's "HaTikvah" ("The Hope"), Mexico's "Mexican National Hymn" (or "Mexicans, When You Hear the War Cry"), France's "Marseillaise," and the "National Anthem of Ghana" are played during independence celebrations.

Aside from these solemn songs are rousing marches, traditional or humorous songs about revolutionary times (for example, "Yankee Doodle" in the United States), and the music and dance traditions of each country.

Special Role of Children, Young Adults

Independence and national days play an important role in educating children about their country's history and culture. Children often participate in plays and pageants that reenact events surrounding independence. They may march in parades and compete in sports during the holidays. Independence days are also family days for picnicking and being outdoors or going to special events, such as rodeos or soccer games.

France

Name of Holiday: Bastille Day

Introduction

Bastille Day has been celebrated as France's national day since 1790, the year following the storming of the Bastille prison by the working-class people of Paris. This event triggered the French Revolution, and is marked each year with impressive military parades, fireworks, and dancing in the streets.

History

During the late eighteenth century in France, life was difficult for most people. King Louis XVI (1754–1793) ruled the country as absolute monarch, meaning the people had no voice in the government. The nation was nearly bankrupt after fighting the French and Indian War (1754–63) and helping the American colonists win their independence from England during the American Revolution (1775–83). Yet the royal family, especially the queen, Marie-Antoinette (1755–1793), kept spending money on lavish clothing, balls and feasts, and endless luxuries. The wealthy nobility and the clergy (bishops, priests, and other officials of the Roman Catholic Church) paid little or no taxes, so the burden of paying for the expenses of government and the country's large debt fell on the working poor and middle classes.

In the French countryside, peasants lived under the feudal system, in which they farmed land for the nobles and in turn received a small house and plot of land for themselves. But a portion of all they grew had to be paid to the landowner, and many other taxes, such as a tax on salt, were added on by the king. They also paid a portion of their earnings to the Church.

The farmer peasants were sometimes obligated to work for free on road projects, bridges, and canals. Landowners controlled the flour mills, bread ovens, and wine presses, and the peasants had to pay to use them. Nobles were the only ones who could hunt, and they could run their horses and hounds anywhere they liked when chasing game, even through a farmer's fields.

In the towns and cities, the middle class, called the *bourgeoisie* (pronounced burzh-wah-ZEE)—made up of businessmen, doctors, lawyers, skilled craftsmen, and merchants—also paid heavy taxes, as did workers in the textile, glass, paper, and other industries.

After a drought destroyed many of the farmers' crops and orchards during the summer of 1788, there came a cold, icy winter. Water mills could not grind wheat into flour because the rivers were frozen, and there was a shortage of bread, a dietary staple for the poor. Many people did not even have firewood because they were not allowed to take wood from the landowners' forests. In the cities, many industrial workers lost their jobs, and prices rose so high they could not afford to provide their families' basic needs. Living conditions became worse and worse for the poor, who made up the majority of France's twenty-six million people.

New ideas about freedom

Adding to the unrest among the working classes were new ideas in Europe

Fireworks light up the sky over the Eiffel Tower in Paris, France, during Bastille Day 1997. Reproduced by permission of AP/Wide World Photos.

about democratic government (government by the people) and basic human rights. French and English writers and philosophers wrote about the equality of all people and rights such as freedom of speech, religion, and the press.

Ideas about self-government were introduced to France by American statesmen Benjamin Franklin and Thomas Jefferson, who served as ambassadors from the colonies. Many of the people with new ideas about the rights of man were French soldiers who had fought with General

George Washington in the American Revolution, including the Marquis de Lafayette (1757–1834), who helped the colonists win their independence from England.

The National Assembly and the Rights of Man

Realizing the seriousness of his country's problems, King Louis XVI called a meeting for May 1789 at his palace in Versailles (pronounced ver-SIGH), near Paris. This would be a meeting of the Estates-General, representatives chosen from the three main social classes—or estates—of France: the clergy (the First Estate), the nobility (the Second Estate), and everyone who was not a member of these two classes (the Third Estate). This type of meeting had not been called by a ruler of France since 1614.

King Louis hoped that by bringing men representing all the people together, a solution could be found to France's problems. But the members of the Estates-General argued for weeks and accomplished nothing. The poor were unfairly represented and were easily outvoted by the nobility and the clergy.

Finally, the Third Estate broke away from the Estates-General and formed the National Assembly, a group similar to the American Continental Congress. They took an oath to keep meeting until the king recognized them as a governing body of France. This oath was called the Tennis Court Oath because the group met in a covered tennis court after the king locked them out of their regular meeting place.

The National Assembly abolished the feudal system, and members wrote the Declaration of the Rights of Man and of the Citizen, which was drafted by Lafayette.

The declaration states the principles of a new government and the "inalienable and sacred rights of man," including the equality of all people, the right to contribute to the forming of laws, the right to express opinions, freedom of speech and the press, the establishing of a police force, equal taxation, equal voting rights (for men; French women did not gain the right to vote until 1945), property rights, and the right to have government officials account for the way they run their offices.

The National Assembly adopted the Declaration of the Rights of Man and of the Citizen on August 26, 1789. Five weeks later, it passed an act changing France from an absolute monarchy to a constitutional monarchy, similar to Great Britain's form of government. This divided the government into executive, legislative, and judicial branches. But about six weeks before the Declaration was adopted, an important event took place in Paris that lit the fuse of the French Revolution.

Storming the Bastille

Between May and July 1789, the French people grew more restless and angry that nothing had been done to improve their living conditions. They feared each day that King Louis would send troops to fire on the people and destroy the National Assembly and its new form of democratic government.

On the morning of July 14, the working people of Paris, inspired by revolutionary speakers, decided to take matters into their own hands. If they wanted to defend themselves, they needed weapons. They found out that the Invalides (pronounced in-vah-LEED), a hospital for retired and wounded soldiers, had a store of some thirty-two thousand muskets. A group of about sixty thousand Parisians stormed the gates of the Invalides and took the weapons. Now all they needed was ammunition, and they knew of one place where enough gunpowder was stored to supply them all—the Bastille.

The Bastille, a four-hundred-year-old stone fortress, was surrounded by a moat, a trench filled with water to prevent entry except by drawbridges that could be raised and lowered. Its walls were one hundred feet high and eight feet thick, with eight massive round towers supporting them. The Bastille had served since the seventeenth century as a prison for those accused of crimes against the king and the state. Many stories were told about the conditions in the prison, but on July 14, 1789, only seven prisoners were held there; others had been released or moved.

The Bastille was overseen by a governor, the Marquis de Launay (pronounced mar-KEE duh loh-NAY), and was defended by eighty-two retired soldiers and thirty-two members of the king's guard, led by a lieutenant. Two days earlier, the king had ordered 250 barrels of gunpowder moved from his poorly guarded arsenal to the Bastille for safety.

Before noon on July 14, hundreds of angry Parisians had gathered outside the Bastille. The townspeople tried to negotiate with de Launay for control of the Bastille, but he refused to give up the fortress. He pulled back his guns and cannons, however, and swore that his men would not fire on the people unless they attacked.

But the crowd, growing larger and more agitated as the minutes passed, want-

ed the Bastille. Some people in the crowd went in through an unguarded courtyard and passageway to the governor's house, then broke down gates and released a drawbridge by chopping at it with axes and hammers. While they were crossing the drawbridge, someone fired shots and the soldiers began firing from the top of the Bastille. Parties of men tried two more times to approach the gates of the Bastille and negotiate with de Launay, but they were fired at in the confusion.

In a nearby hotel, about three hundred more citizens had gathered. They were given muskets taken from the Invalides, and an outspoken patriot named Pierre Hulin persuaded the leaders of sixty-two guards to join in the fight. This well-armed crowd marched to the Bastille and was joined by another group of soldiers. When cannon fire failed to bring down the ironclad walls of the Bastille, the patriots decided to try and blast through the remaining drawbridges and gates. When he saw two cannons pointed at the Bastille's large drawbridge and the pedestrian bridge, de Launay tried to surrender, but the Parisians kept firing.

At 5 P.M., de Launay wrote a note saying he would blow up the Bastille and the surrounding neighborhoods with the gunpowder stored in the cellar unless the revolutionaries accepted his surrender. When the people refused, Hulin prepared to fire the cannon. Just at that moment, retired soldiers inside the Bastille lowered the drawbridge, and the crowd rushed in. The soldiers laid down their arms, and the people rushed to the top of the Bastille to proclaim their victory. The seven prisoners were freed. De Launay was stabbed and beheaded by the angry mob as the patriots marched him through the streets.

Very few soldiers defending the Bastille on July 14 were killed, but about eighty Parisians died and about one hundred were wounded. The crowd seized the gunpowder stored in the cellars of the Bastille. Some was distributed to the revolutionaries and the rest was stored for future use.

After the fall of the Bastille, the people celebrated until dark, firing guns in honor of the conquerors who had taken the fortress. King Louis XVI realized he could not trust his troops to fight the crowds, because most were on the side of the revolutionaries. He gave way to many of their demands, making peace for a short time, but the revolutionaries would continue the struggle for freedom and democracy for another ten years under the motto "Liberty, Equality, Fraternity!"

First Bastille Day celebrations

One year after the fall of the Bastille, on July 14, 1790, the people of Paris held a huge celebration called the Festival of the Federation. On the Champ-de-Mars military parade ground, they built a large amphitheater, an altar to the nation, and a huge arch. Revolutionary soldiers fired their muskets and cannon and proclaimed allegiance to France, the new laws, and to the king, who at that time appeared to accept the constitutional monarchy. The king and queen dressed in the revolutionary colors—blue, white, and red. There was a parade, flag flying, and organ music, and a Catholic high mass was sung. Lafayette spoke about the constitution and the unity of the French people.

After the Revolution

In 1799, military leader Napoléon Bonaparte (1769–1821) set himself up as emperor of France. He led the French army to victory in his conquest of much of western Europe. The French Revolution introduced Europe and much of the world to ideas about nationalism, human rights, and the right of the people to elect those who will make the laws and policies affecting them. Because of this, France became known as a cradle of liberty.

Folklore, Legends, Stories

Like the American Revolution, the French Revolution is associated with many legends that are based on historical fact but have probably been enhanced by writers and storytellers of the day.

A slow process

A popular story is told about the July 14, 1789, storming of the Invalides, where the Parisians took thousands of muskets stored in the cellar before marching on the Bastille. It is said that the day before the march on the military hospital, the governor, fearing the revolutionaries would attempt to steal the muskets, put twenty retired soldiers to work unscrewing the hammers of the muskets so they would be unusable. But the soldiers were on the side of the revolutionaries. After six hours, they had unscrewed only one hammer each, leaving nearly all the muskets ready for use by the patriots.

No, Sire ...

An important legend about the fall of the Bastille says that on the morning of July 15, the day after the Parisians took over the great fortress, a French duke awoke

King Louis XVI at the Palace of Versailles, twelve miles away, and told him what had happened the day before. The king said, "It is a revolt, then." The duke replied, "No, Sire. It is a revolution."

Ideas behind the Revolution

Many of the ideas that started the French Revolution came from Europe's writers, journalists, and philosophers. These new ideas helped create what became known as the Age of Enlightenment. The main idea of this period was that people had a right to determine their own destiny in life.

One French writer whose work had a great influence on the Revolution was Jean-Jacques Rousseau (1712–1778). He wrote about the equality of all men and their right to be represented in government in *The Social Contract* (1762) and *Confessions* (1781; 1788). In *Confessions,* Rousseau refers to a popular myth about Queen Marie Antoinette. When hungry peasants came to the palace demanding bread, she is said to have told King Louis, "Let them eat cake!" Historians say she did not really make this frivolous remark.

Voltaire (pseudonym of François-Marie Arouet; 1694–1778) wrote about the rights of men and freedom of speech, the press, and religion. He was twice imprisoned in the Bastille. The works of the seventeenth-century English writer John Locke (1632–1704), such as his *Two Treatises on Government* (1690), also influenced the thinking of the revolutionaries.

These writers' ideas were reflected in the Declaration of the Rights of Man and of the Citizen. The lawyer Charles de Secondat, the Baron of Montesquieu (1689–1755), influenced the new form of government with his writings about a constitutional monarchy.

Paris was at the center of many of these new ideas, and pamphlets, newspapers, and journals were an important way of getting many different points of view to the people. Therefore, freedom of the press was central to the Revolution. One of most popular journals was *L'Ami du Peuple* (*Friend of the People*), published by Jean-Paul Marat (1743–1793). He encouraged violence in the Revolution and was one of the first revolutionaries to call for the king's death.

Customs, Traditions, Ceremonies

Bastille Day is celebrated throughout France and its territories with parades, fireworks, and dances. It is a joyous, exciting occasion when the French go all out to show their national pride.

Colors on parade in Paris

Paris is famous for its Bastille Day celebrations, and more than a million people come for the event each year. A big attraction is the formal military parade along Paris's major boulevard, the Champs Elysées (pronounced shahnz ay-LEE-zay). The parade features soldiers in dress uniform, tanks and other armored vehicles, marching bands, and dignitaries passing by crowds cheering and waving flags. Helicopters and even Mirage fighter jets fly overhead. A spectacular air show features jet planes flying in formation, with plumes of blue, white, and red smoke stretching out behind. A highlight of the show is a fly-by of the supersonic Concorde jet, which can cruise at speeds of up to 1,330 miles per hour.

Books About the French Revolution

A Tale of Two Cities (1859) by Charles Dickens

The Scarlet Pimpernel (1902) by Baroness Emmuska Orczy

Scaramouche (1921) by Rafael Sabatini

The Glass-Blowers (1963) Daphne Du Maurier

A Place of Greater Safety (1993) by Hilary Mantel

The French flag is flown from downtown buildings and many homes, and at night the entire city is lit up for the festivities. A huge fireworks display in the national colors begins after dark, and people line up for a view along the Seine River.

At the site of the Bastille, a monument to the French Revolution is decorated with French flags, and people gather to hear live bands and dance in the street all night on July 13, the eve of Bastille Day. Fire stations throughout Paris sponsor Firemen's Balls, and Parisian firefighters entertain the guests by dressing in uniform and waiting tables. A huge dinner is served to the crowd. Some firemen provide dance music by playing accordions. Many other organizations also sponsor balls on the eve of Bastille Day.

Bastille Day in other cities

Each city and town in France holds its own colorful Bastille Day celebration. The central features are parades, fireworks, and music and dancing. The town mayor or other dignitary might give a speech in the town square. Nearly every town celebrates with fireworks.

The walled town of Carcassonne in southern France is famous for its two-week Bastille Day festival featuring plays, music and dance, a music and light show, and a spectacular fireworks display. Moving spotlights make the whole town appear to be on fire.

Clothing, Costumes

Clothing played an important part in the French Revolution. People's rights were defined by their social class, and their manner of dress marked them as belonging to a certain group. Queen Marie-Antoinette's love for beautiful and elaborate costumes was part of the monarchy's downfall. It is said that she had more than one hundred new dresses made for her each year before the Revolution, even though France was bankrupt and could not afford the cost.

The working men of Paris became known as the *sans-culottes* (pronounced sahn coo-LOT; without knee-pants), because they wore long trousers instead of the nobility's short, tight satin breeches that came only to the knees. After the Revolution began, it was dangerous to be seen in nobleman's costume, and many men adopted the plain, dark wool clothing of the middle and working classes. They wore long pants and had no lace or gold buttons on their shirts. This plain, dark-colored clothing is a forerunner of the modern-day business suit.

Wealthy women's dress and hairstyles became much more simple. Instead

The French Republican horse guard opens the Bastille Day parade down the Champs Elysées in Paris, July 14, 1998. Paris is famous for its Bastille Day celebrations, and more than a million people come for the event each year. Reproduced by permission of AP/Wide World Photos.

Soldiers of the French Foreign Legion, one of the elite corps of the French army, march down
Paris's Champs Elysées during the military parade celebrating Bastille Day, July 14, 1995.
Reproduced by permission of AP/Wide World Photos.

of high, fluffed hair that imitated the queen's, women wore their hair in curls against their foreheads. Moving away from full, hooped skirts, they wore the flowing, high-waisted dresses of classical Greece, made of plain cloth. Peasant women wore plain skirts and blouses and wooden shoes that allowed them to move about freely.

The revolutionaries became widely recognized by the common red wool caps they wore. Such a cap was called a *bonnet rouge* (red bonnet). For festive occasions such as Bastille Day celebrations, women often wore white dresses with tricolor sashes. They wore tricolor cockades, or hats, while walking in the streets during the Reign of Terror (1793–94) so they could not be mistaken as an enemy of the Revolution.

For Bastille Day celebrations today, the majority of people do not wear special clothing. Those participating in parades or processions may wear uniforms or costumes. Clothing and accessories in blue, white, and red are always appropriate for the celebration.

The Guillotine

The guillotine (pronounced GIH-luh-teen), an instrument for beheading criminals, was widely used during the French Revolution and for many years afterward. France's last king and queen, Louis XVI and Marie-Antoinette, were both guillotined in 1793. The wooden frame with a heavy, tapered blade that supposedly made execution quick and painless was given the nickname "the national razor."

The guillotine was designed by French doctor Joseph-Ignace Guillotin (1738–1814) to replace public torture as a method of execution. Guillotin's invention, designed in 1789 and first used in 1792, put an end to life in less than one second. During the Reign of Terror (1793–94), anyone thought to be critical of the new revolutionary government was put to death. It is estimated that approximately forty thousand people were sent to the guillotine.

The accused rode in open carts and were placed in stocks beneath the blade, face down, with hands tied behind their backs. After the ninety-pound blade fell from a height of more than seven feet, the head rolled into a basket and was held up for the crowd to see.

Foods, Recipes

Bastille Day celebrations are not associated with any particular food. As with the Fourth of July in the United States, however, it is a time for outdoor fun, picnics, and summertime refreshment. Traditionally, families get together for picnics in the park following Bastille Day parades. In Paris, the most popular picnic spot is the Champ-de-Mars, a large, open grassy area that was the site of the first Bastille Day celebration, held on July 14, 1790.

Arts, Crafts, Games

The French painter Jacques-Louis David (1748–1825) was the foremost painter of the French Revolution, recording many of the important events in French history. He served as a member of the National Convention in 1792 and painted a picture of the National Assembly taking the Tennis Court Oath during the summer of 1789. David is famous for his painting of the death of the revolutionary journalist Jean-Paul Marat, who was stabbed by Charlotte Corday, a member of the opposing political party. David also drew a sketch of Marie-Antoinette as she rode in a cart to the guillotine. He was appointed court painter by Emperor Napoléon Bonaparte (1769–1821) in 1804.

Decorating for Bastille Day

A decorating tradition for Bastille Day in towns and villages is to fly the national flag, the Tricolor, from balconies and in front yards, and to deck the house inside and out with fresh flowers, including roses, blue cornflowers, and poppies. Wreaths made of

"The Marseillaise"

Ye sons of France, awake to glory!
Hark! Hark! the people bid you rise!
Your children, wives, and grandsires hoary
Behold their tears and hear their cries.

Shall hateful tyrants, mischief breeding,
With hireling hosts a ruffian band
Affright and desolate the land
While peace and liberty lie bleeding?

CHORUS

To arms, to arms, ye brave!
Th'avenging sword unsheath!
March on, march on, all hearts resolved
On liberty or death.

oak or other green leaves are also popular. Farmers riding into town for Bastille Day parades once decorated their farm wagons and horses with flowers and flags.

Bastille Day fun

In the French countryside, fairs were once very popular on Bastille Day and are still held in many villages. They often feature petting zoos, booths and side shows, obstacle races, greased-pole climbing, and log rolling on rivers. In French cities, a visit to a theme park, zoo, or aquarium is a fun way to spend Bastille Day.

Music, Dance

The French national anthem, "Marseillaise" (pronounced mar-say-YEZ),

was composed during the night and early morning of April 24 and 25, 1792, by Claude-Joseph Rouget de Lisle (1760–1836), a French military captain and composer. He wrote it as a marching song for the revolutionary army, and its original title was "War Song for the Army of the Rhine." Volunteers from the city of Marseilles (pronounced mar-SAY) sang it on their march to Paris on July 30, 1792. They sang with so much emotion that it became known as "The Marseillaise." The First Republic of France adopted the song as the French national anthem in 1795. In 1958, it was made the official national anthem.

Song and dance for the Revolution

More than two thousand songs accompanied popular dances during the Revolution. Many people could not read, so songs became a way of debating and expressing opinions. The streets, cafes, and meeting places were often filled with singing, and the songs had patriotic or humorous lyrics. Supporters of the Revolution and those still loyal to the crown sometimes did verbal battle in song. Crowds gathered around street singers and sang along to songs they knew. Old tunes were often used with new words. People even sang at meetings of the National Assembly.

After the fall of the Bastille, the people celebrated far into the night with song and dance. In August 1792, when revolutionaries attacked the royal palace in Paris, the Tuileries, killing the guards and capturing the royal family, they sang the "Carmagnole" (pronounced car-MAH-nyole). Its refrain says, "Let's dance the Carmagnole! Long live the cannon's roar!" The song is still sung today to celebrate the Revolution and is accompanied by a lively dance.

Today, when people throughout France celebrate Bastille Day, music and dancing is as much a part of the festival as the parades and fireworks. Street dancing goes on in Paris all night to the music of live bands; other towns hold concerts given by orchestras, jazz bands, or popular groups. A large opera house has been built near the site of the Bastille in Paris. Every town and village holds its own Bastille Day dance.

For More Information

Benedict, Kitty C. *The Fall of the Bastille.* Englewood Cliffs, N.J.: Silver Burdett, 1991.

Mulherin, Jenny, ed. *The French Revolution.* New York: Marshall Cavendish, 1991.

Mulvihill, Margaret. *The French Revolution: Bastille and Guillotine.* New York: Gloucester Press, 1989.

Stewart, Gail. *Life During the French Revolution.* San Diego, Calif.: Lucent Books, 1995.

Web sites

"Bastille Day: 14 July the National Holiday." [Online] http://www.premier-ministre.gouv.fr/GB/HIST/FETNAT.HTM (accessed on February 11, 2000).

"Declaration of the Rights of Man and of the Citizen." [Online] http://www.larocheind.com/Declaration.htm (accessed on February 13, 2000).

"Tricolor Flag." [Online] http://www.premier-ministre.gouv.fr/GB/HIST/DRAPEAU.HTM (accessed on February 12, 2000).

Ghana

Name of Holiday: Independence Day

Introduction

Ghana became a leader in Africa when it won its independence from Great Britain on March 6, 1957. With a rich tribal history, Ghana's people were determined to govern themselves and create their own future. Formerly called the Gold Coast, Ghana is named for an ancient African kingdom.

History

A great kingdom called Ouagadou (pronounced WAH-guh-doo) arose in West Africa between the fifth and eleventh centuries. It lay about five hundred miles north of present-day Ghana, south of the Sahara Desert and between the Senegal and Niger Rivers, in the approximate area of the present-day countries of Mauritania, Mali, and Senegal.

Ouagadou was the kingdom of the Soninke (pronounced soh-NIN-kee) people, who controlled the trading of gold that was mined just to the south of their kingdom by the people of Bambuk (pronounced bahm-BOOK). Traders from North Africa and the Middle East crossed the Sahara desert in camel caravans to exchange salt and many other goods for gold.

The word "ghana" means "war chief" in the Soninke language. Expanding as well as defending the rich nation was a duty of the Soninke kings. Because fighting power was so important to the growth of Ouagadou, the term "ghana" gradually came to refer to the nation itself, and Ouagadou became known as the kingdom of Ghana.

The Ashanti nation

About five hundred miles to the south of the ancient kingdom of Ghana, in the valley of the Volta River, lay the forests and plains inhabited by peoples who spoke the Akan (pronounced ah-KAHN) language. This land was also rich in gold, especially the hilly Adanse (pronounced uh-DAHN-say) region. One large group of peoples who had lived in the Adanse region for thousands of years were the Oyoko (pronounced oh-YOH-koh) clan, which would later become the great nation of Ashanti.

By the fifteenth century, traders from the Middle East and Europe had discovered that the forest lands of Adanse contained greater gold fields than any other land in Africa. The Akan peoples traded their gold with Muslims and later with Europeans, chiefly the Portuguese, for goods like iron, salt, weapons, glassware, and cloth. In 1471, the Portuguese were the first Europeans to sail to the West African coast and discover the riches of this land. They called the region *Costa D'Oro* (Gold Coast).

As the Oyoko people grew more powerful and expanded to the north, they named themselves the Ashanti after the sacred grove of the Asantemanso, from which the clan was believed to have originated. The Ashanti used African slaves purchased from the Muslims and the Portuguese to clear land in the forest for building communities and farms and to mine gold, which increased their wealth.

In the mid-1600s, however, the more powerful Denkyira (pronounced dayn-KYEER-uh) people, who lived to the southwest, defeated the Ashanti in battle. The Ashanti could not be free until a wise leader came to power and unified the many villages and clans of the Ashanti into one great kingdom. That leader was Osei Tutu (pronounced OH-say too-too).

Osei Tutu brought the Ashanti together through their common religious beliefs and respect for the *akonnua,* or royal stool, which was believed to represent the spiritual power of Ashanti leaders (see "The Golden Stool of the Ashanti" under "Symbols"). After winning a battle with the Denkyira in 1701, the Ashanti nation became the greatest power in the region. It was one of the world's richest empires.

Great Britain and the Gold Coast Crown Colony

Hoping to gain control of the Ashanti gold fields, the British started a war with the Ashanti and sided with their enemies the Fante (pronounced fahn-TAY). In 1874, after defeating Ashanti warriors in battle, the British looted and burned the Ashanti capital, Kumase. The Ashanti, in return for peace, agreed to let Britain control the Gold Coast.

In 1896, in order to officially disband the Ashante kingdom, a British force marched into Kumase, arrested the new Ashanti ruler, Prempe I, and sent him into exile. In 1900, when a British officer demanded to be given the most sacred symbol of the Ashanti, the Golden Stool, the people were outraged. They once again fought the British but lost to Britain's machine guns and artillery. During the confusion of battle, the Ashanti hid the Golden Stool, preserving it for future kings and for the Ashanti people.

In 1901, Ashanti and the coastal lands belonging to the British became joined as the Gold Coast Crown Colony of Great Britain. Because they believed it was best to use native rulers, the British restored Prempe I to leadership of the Ashanti in 1924.

The push for independence

Under the British, the Gold Coast prospered, largely due to the efforts of the natives. The Ashanti had developed their trade in cocoa beans (used to make chocolate), making the Gold Coast the leading exporter of cocoa in the world. The Ashanti did well in the twentieth century because of their organizational skills and a sense of national unity and pride provided by the Golden Stool. The people were educated, and many often expressed ideas about independence and self-government.

By World War II (1939–45), Ghana had trade unions, writers, and political leaders who believed that their country could grow more if it was not restricted by Britain's trade policies. The Ashanti were strongly behind the move for independence from Great Britain, which began in 1945.

After the war, Britain was weakened economically and could not provide the people of the Gold Coast with the free health care, education, and community services they needed. One sore point involved African soldiers who had fought for Great Britain in World Wars I (1914–18) and II. The African soldiers fought well, but the British would not give them pay and benefits when they returned to the Gold Coast after World War II.

In the summer of 1947, a large group of former soldiers marched through the Gold Coast capital of Accra (pronounced uh-KRAH) to ask the governor for the money and benefits owed them for serving in the military. British police fired on the men, and the angry citizens of Accra rose up against the colonial government.

Others throughout the colony joined the revolt, and the British army, navy, and air force attacked the Gold Coast natives to stop the uprising. Many civilians were killed or wounded. Shortly afterward, two new political organizations—the Ashanti Youth Association and the United Gold Coast Convention (UGCC)—helped move the people toward independence.

Kwame Nkrumah, leader with a plan

In 1947, Kwame Nkrumah (pronounced KWAH-me en-KROO-muh; 1909–1972), a Gold Coast native who had gone to college in the United States and Great Britain, was appointed to the powerful position of secretary-general of the UGCC. His slogan was "Self-Government Now."

In 1948, after his release from a short stay in prison for organizing protest demonstrations, Nkrumah founded the Convention People's Party (CPP), which demanded the Gold Coast's immediate independence from Britain through nonviolent means. In 1949, Nkrumah started a civil disobedience movement that again got him arrested by the British.

With so many Gold Coast citizens behind Nkrumah and the CPP, the colonial government knew it could not stop the movement for freedom. Britain could not afford to go to war with the African colony over independence. At the same time, the colonial leaders wanted to be sure that independence was what the majority of Gold Coast citizens wanted. They insisted on elections to determine the popular support of the CPP.

Between 1951 and 1957, the change from colonial rule to democratic government gradually took place. In February 1951, the CPP won a majority of seats in the Gold Coast National Assembly in the first general

Kwame Nkrumah, in ceremonial robes with his sword-bearer in front of him and his wife at his side, on his way to open Ghana's second parliament in 1965. Within a year he would fall from power. Reproduced by permission of AP/Wide World Photos.

election. Nkrumah was released from prison to become the "leader of government business." In March 1952, he was made prime minister of the Gold Coast, making him the first African-born prime minister of a British colony. In 1954 and 1956, in elections called by British officials, the CPP again won by a large majority of votes.

On August 3, 1956, the National Assembly unanimously passed a motion calling for independence. In March 1957, Britain agreed to release the Gold Coast to independent government, making it the first European country with territories in Africa to do so. Nkrumah chose to rename the Gold Coast "Ghana," after the great kingdom to the north that had flourished one thousand years before. The borders of the new nation correspond closely with the borders of the Ashanti kingdom at its height, and Akan-speaking peoples make up nearly half of Ghana's population.

March 6, 1957: Ghana is free

At midnight on March 5, 1957, Kwame Nkrumah began a speech proclaiming Ghana a free nation. He told his fellow countrymen:

At long last the battle has ended ... and thus Ghana, your beloved country, is free forever.... I am depending upon the millions of the country, the chiefs and people, to help me to reshape the destiny of this country. We are going to see that we create our own African personality and identity.... We again rededicate ourselves in the struggle to emancipate other countries in Africa, for our independence is meaningless unless it is linked up with the total liberation of the African continent.

On March 6, 1957, Ghana declared its freedom as an independent nation within the British Commonwealth, with Nkrumah still prime minister. Within ten years of Ghana's independence, all other British colonies in Africa except Rhodesia had also gained their freedom.

Ghana celebrates independence

A great ceremony was held on March 6, 1957, to usher in Ghana's independence. All eyes were on this country as it became the first African nation south of the Sahara Desert to gain freedom from colonial rule. People in the United States who were working for civil rights for African Americans were interested in Ghana as a model of black freedom, self-sufficiency, and pride.

Kwame Nkrumah was a hero to black people throughout the world. Many newspapers in the United States gave wide coverage to Ghana's independence and to this first celebration. One newspaper held an essay contest for American high school and college students and sent the winners to Accra to attend the independence celebration on March 6.

U.S. president Dwight D. Eisenhower (1890–1969) and his administration hoped that Ghana could help fight the threat of communism in Africa by declaring a democratic government and forming an alliance with the Western world. He sent vice president Richard Nixon (1913–1994) and a delegation to Ghana to attend the ceremonies. Nkrumah invited black leaders from all over Africa and the world to attend. Eleven black leaders from the United States alone attended. Great Britain's Duchess of Kent was also present.

In addition to all the speeches and handshaking, the most solemn moment came when the British flag, the Union Jack, was lowered and Ghana's flag, the Black Star, was raised. The biggest celebration was in Accra, the capital, but the same flag ceremony took place in cities and towns throughout Ghana. People all over the nation shouted, "Freedom!"

Years after independence

On July 1, 1960, Ghana became a republic, with Nkrumah as its president. After independence, Ghana's economic growth and social change was rapid and exciting. Under Nkrumah, the government built roads, schools, hospitals, factories, and homes and started the Volta River Project. Lake Volta, the world's largest artificial lake, was created when the Akosombo hydroelectric dam was built on the Volta River in 1964. The government also established an airline, improved railways, and encouraged foreign investment.

Nkrumah falls from power

By 1964, Nkrumah had assumed more and more power in Ghana and even tried to take power from the Ashanti king and other traditional rulers. He declared Ghana a one-party state and named himself president for life. On February 24, 1966, while Nkrumah was on a visit to China, Ghana's army and police led a coup d'état (military takeover) of his government, the first of five coups in Ghana between 1966 and 1999. Nkrumah was forbidden to return to Ghana. He died in Guinea in 1972 but was buried with honors in his native village in Ghana.

Folklore, Legends, Stories

The Ashanti people of Ghana have always had a strong sense of their history, and many folktales and legends that were passed down for generations by storytellers have now been written down.

The Ashanti woman who called for war

Queen Mother Yaa Asantewaa (pronounced YAH-ah ah-sahn-tay-WAH-ah) was a brave Ashanti woman who lived during the late nineteenth and early twentieth centuries. After the British sent King Prempe I into exile in 1896, the Ashanti held a meeting to decide how to get him back. Some of the men did not want to make war on the British. But Yaa Asantewaa told them, "If you, the men of Ashanti will not go forward, then we, the women, will. I shall call upon my fellow women. We will fight the white men. We will fight till the last of us falls in the battlefields."

These brave words roused the men to fight, and Yaa Asantewaa and the men and women of Ashanti fought together against the British, with the Queen Mother often leading the battles. In 1900, when a British military leader asked to be given the Golden Stool so that he might sit on it, the Ashanti were enraged. Yaa Asantewaa and her people led an attack on the British fort in Kumase. The British had more modern weapons and more troops, so the Ashanti were defeated. The Golden Stool, however, remained hidden and was kept from the British. Yaa Asantewaa and others were sent into exile.

Customs, Traditions, Ceremonies

Events for celebrating Ghana's independence sometimes begin a week before and continue a week after Independence Day. Although independence celebrations have faded somewhat since 1957, many of the same activities continue today. Some of these are the hoisting of the flags at Kwame Nkrumah Circle in Accra, the showing of historical films on television, dramatic reenactments of Ghana's independence story, and lectures about independence and government on radio and TV. A Military Open Day for schoolchildren is held at military forts and bases, and military exercises and arms displays thrill crowds in major cities.

Sporting events are also popular Independence Day activities. Some schools give gymnastics displays. Soccer games are held in Accra and Kumase, and there are athletic events and boxing matches in many cities.

Fireworks are a big part of Ghana's Independence Day celebrations, as they are in the United States and most other nations. Other events include National Honors and Awards days, candlelight processions, cultural displays, and music and dancing in the streets.

Islam is a major religion in Ghana, and mosques (pronounced MOSKS) hold a Muslim Day of Prayers for the Nation on the Friday following March 6. Friday is the holiest day of the week for Muslims. Musical festivals and outdoor programs are sometimes held at mosques throughout Ghana. Christian churches also hold special Independence Day services. A National Thanksgiving Service is often held to close out the independence celebrations.

Independence Day parades

As in France, Israel, Mexico, and the United States, Ghana celebrates its Independence Day with parades. The parade ground at Independence Square in Accra is the site of the largest parade, but parades are held throughout Ghana for independence celebrations. Ghana's schoolchildren and veterans are among special groups that march in their own Independence Day parades in Accra and all regional capitals.

Clothing, Costumes

Most modern-day Ghanaians wear Western-style clothing for everyday life, especially in the larger cities. Some people, however, choose to wear traditional clothing for Independence Day and other festivals, and for special occasions within the family.

The traditional dress of Ghana probably originated in Kumase, the capital city of the Ashanti Empire, in the mid-1700s. Women wrapped a long piece of cloth around their waists to make a skirt that came to the knees. This garment was called a *ntoma* (pronounced en-TOH-mah), or "cloth." Child carriers were made by wrapping cloth around the upper body to make a pocket for the child on the mother's back. Men draped a large piece of cloth over one shoulder and let it fall to their ankles.

Today, some men and women still wear ntomas, often made of *kente* (pronounced KEN-tay) cloth. Women wear a matching blouse called a *kaba* (pronounced KAH-bah) and a wrap. Kente cloth is considered the national dress of Ghana and is the most popular clothing for Independence Day and other festivals, weddings, and naming ceremonies.

Foods, Recipes

As in most of West Africa, the yam or plantain (a type of banana) dish called *fufu* is a favorite dish in Ghana. Fufu is made from boiled yams that are pounded and shaped into balls. A yam dish called *oto* is served with hard-boiled eggs for breakfast on festival mornings.

Arts, Crafts, Games

Kente cloth is probably Ghana's most well-known craft product. The patterns and colors of this fine cloth are popular throughout the world. The weaving of kente cloth began in the Ashanti empire during the 1600s. According to legend, two Ashanti men watched a spider weaving its web in the forest and decided it was similar to the way the people wove mats from plant fibers. They developed a loom to weave cloth in this manner. The word "kente" comes from the term "kenten," meaning "basket."

The Ashanti king saw how beautiful the cloth was and declared it the royal fabric. From that day, weavers made kente cloth from silk and it was worn only by kings and queens for special ceremonies. Today, it is often worn at national holidays, such as Independence Day.

Oto and Eggs

Ingredients
2 cups mashed potatoes, mashed yams,
  or sweet potatoes

2 tablespoons grated onions

1 tomato, peeled and diced

¾ cup oil (palm oil if possible)

6 hard-boiled eggs

½ teaspoon each, salt and pepper

Directions

1. Fry onions in oil until soft, adding salt and pepper.

2. Add tomatoes, mixing and frying for 2 to 3 minutes. Remove from heat.

3. Mash the yolks from 2 of the eggs, then stir into the onion mixture. Stir this "gravy" into the mashed yams or potatoes and mix well.

4. Empty the *oto* into a serving bowl and place remaining whole boiled eggs on top.

Imitation kente cloth is mass produced in many countries by printing kente patterns on ordinary cotton cloth. Authentic kente cloth, however, is hand-woven on a loom from cotton and silk yarn, in bright colors and geometric designs. It is woven in long, four-inch-wide strips, which are then sewn together to make big pieces of cloth that are worn draped over the body. Kente cloth has traditionally been woven by men, but today many women participate in the process by sewing the long strips together and selling the cloth.

Each kente design has a symbolic meaning, and each pattern is unique, representing African history and culture. Kente patterns can reveal where a person is from and sometimes their social status. African Americans today wear kente cloth to renew a connection with their African homeland and to show appreciation for the artistic talent of the African people.

Music, Dance

Music provided by drums, horns, and stringed instruments have been a part of Ghana's culture for centuries. The *kora* is a traditional West African stringed instrument played by *griots* (pronounced GREE-ohz), or storytellers, who pass on the history of the people.

Traditional African drumming and ceremonial and religious dancing are an important part of Ghana's many festivals throughout the year. Music and dancing in the streets or at special parties make up a big part of Ghana's Independence Day celebrations.

Highlife: The popular music of Ghana

A musical style called "highlife" is associated with twentieth-century Ghana more than any other. It is a staple of festival celebrations, including Independence Day. Highlife is a combination of West African rhythms and the music of European, Caribbean, and American dance orchestras and big bands of the early 1900s. Highlife was named for the upper-class lifestyle of the people who went to clubs where the music was played.

One of the most popular highlife musicians of the 1930s to 1950s was E. T. Mensah, nicknamed the King of Highlife. Kwame Nkrumah, first prime minister and the "father of Ghanaian independence," considered highlife a symbol of Ghana's culture, and he often had a highlife band travel with him on national business.

Ghana's national anthem

Independence Day in Ghana is an occasion for singing the *National Anthem of Ghana:*

God Bless our homeland Ghana,
And make our nation great and
strong,
Bold to defend forever the cause of
Freedom and of Right.
Fill our hearts with true humility,
Make us cherish fearless honesty,
And help us to resist oppressor's rule
With all our will and might for ever-
more.

Special Role of Children, Young Adults

On Ghana's Independence Day, children have a chance to show their skills in sports such as gymnastics. Groups of schoolchildren dress in school uniforms and march in Independence Day parades for local dignitaries.

For More Information

Boateng, Faustine Ama. *Asante*. New York: Rosen, 1996.

Koslow, Philip. *Ancient Ghana: The Land of Gold.* New York: Chelsea House, 1995.

Koslow, Philip. *Asante: The Gold Coast.* New York: Chelsea House, 1996.

Wepman, Dennis. *Africa: The Struggle for Independence.* New York: Facts on File, 1993.

Web sites

"Culture and Tradition: Republic of Ghana." [Online] http://www.ghana.gov.gh/cultra.html (accessed on February 12, 2000).

"Ghana Virtual Journey." [Online] http://www.ontheline.org.uk/explore/journey/ghana/print.htm (accessed on February 12, 2000).

"Ghana's Flag, National Pledge, Anthem, and Coat of Arms." [Online] http://users.erols.com/johnston/pledge.htm (accessed on February 12, 2000).

Israel

Name of Holiday: Yom Ha'atzmaut

Introduction

The story of the attempt to establish a unified Jewish homeland is as old as the history of the Jewish people. Time and again they were driven from their homeland in Israel, but they never gave up hope of regaining the land they believe was promised to them by God. When the Jewish state of Israel was established on May 14, 1948, Jewish people from all over the world began returning to Israel. In spite of ongoing conflict over the land with neighboring peoples, Jews in Israel celebrate Israeli Independence Day, or Yom Ha'atzmaut (pronounced YOME HOTZ-moat), with parades, picnics, and fireworks each year.

History

Judaism is the religion of the ancient Hebrews and the modern Jews. Its development began about four thousand years ago near present-day Israel (then known as Canaan; pronounced KAY-nuhn), in the Middle East, along the eastern coast of the Mediterranean Sea. Much of the ancient history of the Jewish people is recorded in the Hebrew Bible (the Old Testament books of the Christian Bible).

According to the biblical book of Genesis, Abraham, called the father of the Jews, promised God that he would worship and be faithful only to Him. In return, God promised to give the land of Canaan, "a land flowing with milk and honey," to Abraham and his descendants (Genesis 17:8; Exodus 3:7–8).

Abraham's grandson Jacob later became the leader of the Jews. According to the biblical account, Jacob wrestled with an angel, who gave him the name Israel ("one who strives with God"; Genesis 32:28). His followers became known as the Children of Israel.

Servitude in Egypt

In the seventeenth century B.C., a great famine forced many of the Israelites to migrate south to Egypt. There they prospered for a time, tending their herds of cattle. Eventually, however, a cruel pharaoh, or king, came to power. Fearing the Jews were becoming too numerous and prosperous, he decreed that all newborn Jewish males be drowned in the Nile River. He made the rest of the Jewish population his slaves.

"Let my people go"

During the thirteenth century B.C., after the Israelites had been enslaved for some 430 years, the Bible says God chose the prophet Moses to lead the Israelites out of Egypt to Canaan, the Promised Land. Moses gave the pharaoh God's command: "Let my people go, that they may serve me." The pharaoh refused, and God caused ten disasters to fall upon the Egyptians before the ruler set the Israelites free (Exodus 7:14–12:32).

Moses first led the Children of Israel to Mount Sinai, where the Bible says God gave Moses the Ten Commandments and other laws to live by. Leaving Mount Sinai, they came to the southern end of Canaan, and Moses sent men out to scout the Promised Land. Some of the men reported that the land was populated by giants who would destroy them, causing the Israelites to rebel. Because of their rebellion and lack of faith in being able to win the Promised Land, God made them wander in the wilderness for forty years (Joshua 5:6) before they could enter the land promised to Abraham and his descendants.

The kingdom of Israel

After entering Canaan, the Israelites began to gradually conquer the region from the various groups living there. They established the kingdom of Israel in about 1020 B.C., with Saul as their first king. About 1000 B.C., the Israelite leader David recaptured the city of Jerusalem from a people called the Jebusites and made it the capital of his kingdom. Jerusalem was also called "Zion," after a Jebusite stronghold in the city, and "the City of David." It was surrounded by valleys on three sides and had a good water supply, making it an an excellent fortress city.

Jerusalem became the center of Jewish life for the next two thousand years. The country thrived and expanded under King David and his son King Solomon. Under King Solomon, the Israelites became a major power in the region. Solomon brought about prosperity by developing

Moses, kneeling on Mount Sinai, receiving the Ten Commandments from God. After the Israelites had been enslaved for more than four hundred years, Moses led the Israelites out of Egypt. Reproduced by permission of Archive Photos, Inc.

such enterprises as copper mining and lead smelting. His crowning achievement was the building, in about 960 B.C., of a magnificent temple in Jerusalem. The temple became the political and spiritual center of the Jewish people.

Babylonian conquest

The Babylonians (inhabitants of the area that is today southern Iraq) under King Nebuchadnezzar (pronounced NEH-byuh-kuhd-NEH-zur) captured Jerusalem in 586 B.C. They plundered and then destroyed Solomon's temple and exiled many of the Israelites, which some historians say marks the beginning of the Jewish Diaspora (pronounced dye-AS-puh-ruh), or the breaking up and scattering of the Jewish people. Tens of thousands of Israelites were taken to Babylon. In Psalms 137:1, 5–6, they swore never to forget Jerusalem:

> By the rivers of Babylon, we sat and wept
> When we remembered Zion....
> If I forget you, O Jerusalem,
> Let my right hand forget her cunning.
> If I do not remember you, let my tongue cleave to the roof of my mouth.

In about 538 B.C., when the Persians (inhabitants of the area that is present-day Iran) defeated the Babylonian Empire, some fifty thousand Jews began returning to Jerusalem. They built a second temple at the site of the one destroyed by the Babylonians.

Greek influence

Alexander the Great (356–323 B.C.), ruler of Greece, conquered the region in about 332 B.C. Upon his death, one of his lieutenants ruled the area from Syria. Because Syria was under Greek control, Israel gradually came under Greek influence. The Jews finally revolted when the rulers tried to restrict the practice of Judaism and Hellenize them, or make them adopt the Greek language and culture.

The final straw was the attempt by the Syrians to turn the temple in Jerusalem into a house of worship for the Greek god Zeus. A band of Jewish patriots known as the Maccabees (pronounced MA-kuh-beez) drove the Syrian army out of Jerusalem and later established Jewish control over all of Palestine.

Roman rule

In about 63 B.C., the Romans conquered the area. King Herod came to power in 37 B.C. Under his rule, Israel prospered. Herod refurbished the temple and built new cities and fortresses, including a fortress at Masada.

After King Herod's death in 4 B.C., the Jews came to resent the oppressive Roman rule. They revolted in A.D. 66; it took the Romans four years to put down the rebellion. The Romans tore down the second temple in A.D. 70, destroyed the city, and again dispersed much of the Jewish population. Josephus Flavius, a histori-an living at the time, wrote that the Romans killed hundreds of thousands of Jews and sold thousands more into slavery.

To wipe out any vestige of Jewish rule, the Romans renamed the region Palestine. The name Palestine comes from the Greek *Palaistina,* which means "the Land of the Philistines." The Philistines lived in the area during the time of King David. The Jews of Israel would not be independent again for some two thousand years.

The Christian "Holy Land"

The Roman emperor Constantine the Great (ruled 306–37) converted to Christianity in the early part of the fourth century. Christianity is a religion founded by Jesus Christ (c. 6 B.C.–c. A.D. 30). As a result, Palestine, where Jesus Christ had lived and preached, became "the Holy Land" for Christians.

Many churches and monasteries were established at major holy sites, especially in Jerusalem and Bethlehem, the birthplace of Jesus. The Christians blamed the Jews for Jesus' death because it was the Jewish high priests who had condemned him to die. With the land of Israel under Christian domination, the Jews lost many of their rights, such as the right to hold office or serve in the army.

An Islamic "holy city"

In about 640 B.C., the Islamic armies of Caliph Omar (c. 586–644) captured most of the Middle East, which they would rule for more than four centuries. Islam is a religion founded by the prophet Muhammad (c. 570–632). The followers of Islam, called Muslims, believe that Muhammad ascended to heaven from Jerusalem. Therefore, Jerusalem became a holy city to them, as well.

The first Muslim rulers allowed Jews to resettle in Jerusalem. The Jews had to pay special taxes, however, for the protection of their lives and property and religious practice. Under later Muslim rulers, additional restrictions were added against non-Muslims, including heavy taxes on farms. As a result, many Jews were forced to leave Palestine. By the end of the eleventh century, the Jewish population had declined considerably.

During this period, Christians also were persecuted by the Muslims, who destroyed the Church of the Holy Sepulchre, a Christian shrine. In about 1070, Muslim leaders began to bar Christian pilgrims from entering Jerusalem, setting the stage for the Crusades, a series of bloody campaigns to end Muslim control of Palestine.

The Crusades

In 1095, Pope Urban II called for Christians to take back the Holy Land from the Muslims. Ragtag bands of religious soldiers called Crusaders swept through Europe and into the Middle East. They captured Jerusalem in 1099 and slaughtered or exiled large numbers of both Muslims and Jews. The Crusaders would rule the area for two centuries.

With their conquest, the Crusaders opened transportation routes from Europe to the Holy Land. These routes became popular with Christians who wanted to make pilgrimages to the Holy Land. The routes also became popular with the increasing number of Jews seeking to return to their homeland.

Decline of Palestine

The Mamluks, an Egyptian military class, drove the Crusaders out of the Holy Land in the late thirteenth century. Because the Mamluks were defending Syria against invaders from Asia and were engaged in a power struggle at home, Palestine was neglected and began a period of economic and cultural decline. By the end of the Middle Ages (500–1500), Palestine had become a wasteland, and the Jewish population was living in poverty. Christian pilgrims continued to arrive, however, as well as large numbers of Jews who wanted to return to their homeland or were expelled from other countries.

Ottoman rule

The Ottoman Empire was a large empire that controlled parts of Asia, Africa, and Europe. It was founded in the thirteenth century and dissolved in 1918, at the end of World War I. The Turks of the Ottoman Empire conquered the Holy Land in the early 1500s and would rule Palestine for the next four centuries. The Ottoman ruler Suleyman the Magnificent (ruled 1520–66) is credited with returning prosperity to the land, which stimulated more Jewish immigration.

By the nineteenth century, European powers started to help make peace in the region. To that end, many Western countries opened consulates, or offices that represent the interests of a foreign country, in Jerusalem. In 1838, Great Britain opened a consulate and proclaimed itself a defender of the Jews.

The Zionist movement

Since they were first displaced by the Babylonians and Romans, Jews throughout the world have prayed that their people would return to Israel one day. Continual persecution of Jews in Europe fueled the desire even more. Attempts to rebuild the

Jewish state are known as Zionism, after Zion, another name for Jerusalem. The hope of Zionism was for a homeland where Jews could be free of oppression.

The first entirely Jewish colony was established in Israel at Petah Tikva in 1878, and marked the renewal of Jewish nationalism (loyalty to a nation or culture). During the 1880s, more and more Jews fled to Israel because they were being persecuted and massacred in Russia and other countries. The newcomers settled in existing communities or built their own agricultural centers. Such waves of Jewish immigration are called *aliyah* (pronounced ah-LEE-yah), meaning "ascent to the land."

In 1894, the Austrian journalist Theodor Herzl (1860–1904) covered the trial of the French Jewish officer Alfred Dreyfus, who was falsely accused of treason and convicted. Herzl was stunned by the anti-Jewish feelings of the French people when many in the courtroom yelled out "Down with the Jews!" He realized that Jews could escape persecution only if they had their own homeland, and he began advocating such a homeland in his writings. He also organized the First Zionist Congress in Basel, Switzerland, in 1897.

World War I

With the advent of World War I (1914–18), Great Britain sought the help of the Jews and the Arabs in defeating the Ottoman Empire. In doing so, it made conflicting assurances to both peoples regarding homelands in Palestine. The Jews were led to believe that one day they would have their own country, just as the countries of Jordan, Syria, Lebanon, and Iraq had been created for the Arabs. In its 1917 Balfour Declaration, Britain stated that it supported the "establishment in Palestine of a national home for Jewish people."

After the war, Great Britain was ordered by the League of Nations (the forerunner of the United Nations) to govern Palestine. Jewish immigration to Israel rapidly increased. By 1939, almost 430,000 Jews were living in Palestine, accounting for 25 percent of Palestine's population.

The Arabs in Palestine grew more and more resentful, believing Jewish immigration threatened their jobs and their land. The anger soon exploded into riots and violence. To calm the Arabs, Britain withdrew its support for a Jewish homeland in 1939. Fighting between Jews and Arabs intensified.

World War II and the Holocaust

During World War II (1939–45), Nazi German leader Adolf Hitler (1889–1945) and his army attempted to exterminate the Jews of Europe, sending another great flood of Jewish immigrants to Palestine. The British, however, tried to control the wave of Jewish immigrants in order to prevent more conflict with the Arab population. With the door to Palestine shut, much of the Jewish population of Europe was doomed to die. During this episode in history, referred to as the Holocaust, millions of Jews and other people considered enemies of Nazi Germany were tortured, starved, gassed, burned, and buried in mass graves.

In 1948, spurred on by the horrors of the Holocaust, the United Nations decreed that Palestine be divided into two countries, one Arab and one Jewish. The Jews quickly agreed to the plan, but the Arabs resisted it. The Jews, unwilling to wait any longer, proclaimed the state of

The flag of the newly proclaimed Jewish state of Israel blows in the breeze, May 15, 1948.
Reproduced by permission of AP/Wide World Photos.

Israel on May 14, 1948. It was the first Jewish state in nineteen hundred years.

Israel fights to survive

At 5:25 A.M. on May 15, the day after Israel declared its independence, the first Arab bombs, dropped by Egypt, fell on the new country's capital of Tel Aviv. Iraq, Lebanon, Syria, and Transjordan (Jordan) joined in the attack. A bloody Israeli War for Independence was fought. At the same time, Holocaust survivors and other Jews from around the world flooded into Israel.

Hundreds of former British soldiers, a few thousand Jewish "underground" forces who had been agitating for independence, and thousands of Jewish settlers fought valiantly. Their battle cry was "Ein Breiera!" ("No choice!"), meaning no choice but to fight for the life of the country. Israel won the war, the first of five that occurred into the 1980s. It also gained control over half of the area the United Nations had planned to set aside for the new Arab state.

The first Independence Day celebration

Israel's first Independence Day celebration was quiet and private. Out of fear, the people who were creating Israel's Declaration of Independence decided not to declare statehood publicly. They were afraid that the British—who still were technically in power in Israel—might try to prevent Israel from declaring independence. They also were worried that Arab states might move up plans to attack.

A one-page invitation was sent out by messenger on the morning of the declaration. Those who were invited were urged not to disclose the contents of the invitation or the time of the meeting. Guests were asked to arrive at 3:30 P.M. and advised: "Dress: dark festive attire."

This secrecy was not enough to prevent hundreds of people from gathering outside the meeting hall in Tel Aviv. Thousands of others listened to the broadcast on the Voice of Israel radio station.

Inside the meeting hall, there were mostly newspaper editors and correspondents. Other guests included representatives of Jewish organizations, including the Jewish Agency and the World Zionist Organization, chief rabbis, political leaders, and other public and cultural personalities. At 4:00 P.M., David Ben-Gurion (1886–1973), a Polish-born leader active in the Zionist movement, banged a wooden gavel to open the meeting. Spontaneously, the crowd rose and began singing "HaTikva" ("The Hope"), Israel's national anthem.

Ben-Gurion proceeded to read the preamble to the declaration, explaining the background for independence and the history of the Jewish people. He then got to the heart of the document:

> Accordingly, we the members of the National Council, representing the Jewish People in Palestine and the World Zionist Movement, have met together in solemn assembly today, the day of termination of the British Mandate for Palestine; and by virtue of the natural and historic right of the Jewish People and the Resolution of the General Assembly of the United Nations, we hereby proclaim the establishment of the Jewish State in Palestine, to be called Medinat Yisrael [the State of Israel].

Cheering, applauding, and crying, the crowd rose. After Ben-Gurion read the rest of the declaration, the twenty-five signed the document. Accompanied by the seventy-member Palestine Philharmonic Orchestra, the crowd again rose and began singing the "HaTikva." Ben-Gurion then declared: "The State of Israel is established. This meeting is adjourned."

Folklore, Legends, Stories

The long history of the Jewish people is well documented in their sacred books, including the Old Testament of the Bible. Jewish legends are also well preserved as they are orally passed on from generation to generation. One of the greatest legends of the Jewish faith is that when God created the world, he made Jerusalem the center of the universe and the gateway to heaven. According to Jews, all prayers to God go through Jerusalem.

Many Jewish sacred stories tell of miraculous events. These stories serve to remind the Jewish people that they are blessed by God even during trying and horrible times. One such story involves a young David, who eventually became the first great king of all Israel. The story is about a boy who defeats a giant, but it can also be interpreted as the story of a people who survived against impossible odds.

David, the future king of Israel, slaying the Philistine giant Goliath. Many Jewish sacred stories serve to remind the Jewish people that they are blessed even during trying and horrible times. Reproduced by permission of Archive Photos, Inc.

David and Goliath

During the reign of King Saul (c. 1020–1000 B.C.), the Israelites were at war with the Philistines. During one major battle, the two armies were camped on opposite sides of the Valley of Elah, near present-day Jerusalem. Each morning, a Philistine giant named Goliath, who was about ten feet tall, descended into the valley and challenged any Israelite man to do battle with him. The giant wore a bronze helmet and a coat of mail weighing 150 pounds. The head of his spear weighed 19 pounds. The men in Saul's army were terrified.

As Goliath was taunting the Israelites, a shepherd boy named David (Hebrew for "beloved") arrived at the camp.

David had been sent by his father to carry bread and cheese to his brothers, who were in the army. When David heard the giant's taunts and saw how afraid the Israelites were, he told Saul that he would fight Goliath. The boy was confident because he had previously fought bears and lions that attacked his sheep. Saul was reluctant, but finally agreed.

Saul gave David his armor, but David was too small to walk in it, so he removed it. He tried to carry a sword, but again, he was too small. Instead, David gathered five smooth pebbles from a nearby stream and put them in his pouch. With his staff in one hand and his sling in the other, David approached the giant. When

Goliath saw how young and small David was and that his only weapons were a staff and sling, he mocked him and said: "Am I a dog, that you come at me with sticks?" He then cursed David and his God and said, "Come to me, and I will give your flesh to the birds of the air and to the wild animals of the field."

David replied, "You come to me with sword and spear and javelin; but I come to you in the name of the Lord of hosts, the God of the armies of Israel, whom you have defied. This very day the Lord will deliver you into my hand, and I will strike you down and cut off your head." As the giant drew nearer, David ran to meet him. He took a stone from his pouch, put it in his sling, and hit the giant in the forehead. Goliath fell face-first to the ground. David ran to him, grabbed his sword, and cut off his head. The Philistines fled.

Customs, Traditions, Ceremonies

Independence Day in Israel is heralded by the sound of *shofars,* ram's horns that are blown like trumpets. The festivities include fireworks displays, military air and naval shows, picnics and barbecues, and nighttime celebrations with lots of singing and dancing. Jews throughout the world who still hope to one day live in Israel close their holiday celebrations with the shout, "Next year in Jerusalem!"

A day to remember the war dead

Because Israel has lost millions of its people to war, the day before Independence Day commemorates individuals who were killed in war time. Some say Memorial Day (Yom Ha'Zikaron) is observed the day before Independence Day to remind people of the cost of independence. Others point to the Jewish philosophy that people should always remember the times of sorrow along with good times.

On the morning of Memorial Day, sirens sound throughout Israel, and everything comes to a sudden halt—including people and cars—for a two-minute period of silence to remember the dead. Many people also visit cemeteries during the day to pay respect to those killed in war. Television and radio stations broadcast stories and films of famous battles. At nightfall on Memorial Day, the sirens sound again and twelve torches, representing the twelve biblical tribes of Israel, are lit in Jerusalem to mark the end of Memorial Day and the beginning of Independence Day.

A time to celebrate

At sundown on Independence Eve, the country stops grieving and begins to celebrate Independence Day. Public buildings light up with strings of colored lights. Accompanied by live bands or recorded music, people dance in the streets, sometimes until morning. The surrounding hills glow with the lights of bonfires. Many families feast, sing old Hebrew songs, and tell stories late into the night.

Independence Day is celebrated much like the Fourth of July in the United States—with barbecues, picnics, and a lot of noisy fun. In Tel Aviv, Jerusalem, and other cities, revelers go downtown to enjoy the holiday spirit. They take to the streets, throwing sparklers and blowing plastic whistles while loudspeakers blare popular music.

Israeli children play on an army tank at a display of military equipment during Israel's Independence Day festivities in Jerusalem in 1999. Reproduced by permission of AP/Wide World Photos.

A time for unity

Even in times of conflict, Israelis try to come together on Independence Day. In 1988, for example, there was a Palestinian uprising in the Israeli-occupied West Bank and Gaza Strip, and a war between Iran and Iraq threatened to engulf the entire region. The Jewish nation, however, still celebrated its Independence Day.

Most Israelis tend to become one big family on Independence Day. Orthodox (Jews who adhere to strict religious practices) and secular (nonreligious) Jews try to forget their differences and celebrate their nation's statehood. They proudly wave Israeli flags and sing and dance in the streets, sometimes all night long. They also have a strange custom of bopping friends and strangers on the head with plastic hammers during independence celebrations. Another tradition is to spray shaving cream and cans of plastic string on passersby.

Military displays

Many Israelis view a televised military pageant, that includes poking light-hearted fun at military life and soldiers complaining of ill treatment by their superior officers. *Spitfires*, vintage planes from

Falafel

Ingredients

1 cup canned chickpeas (garbanzo beans), drained

⅔ cup fine bread crumbs

1 large clove garlic

½ teaspoon salt

½ teaspoon pepper

1 teaspoon ground cumin

1 tablespoon chopped fresh parsley

2 eggs

1 cup vegetable oil plus 2 tablespoons

2 tablespoons lemon juice

Directions

1. In a food processor, mix the chickpeas, bread crumbs, garlic, salt, pepper, cumin, and parsley.

2. Add the 2 eggs, 2 tablespoons of oil, and 2 tablespoons of lemon juice and mix well. Form the mixture into about 15 balls.

3. Heat the remaining oil until it begins to bubble.

4. With a long-handled slotted spoon, drop the balls in a few at a time and fry until golden brown. Drain on paper towels.

5. You can eat the falafel balls by themselves, or you can place them in a piece of pita bread and add sliced tomatoes and cucumbers.

---

the 1948 War for Independence, do fly-bys along with modern-day F-15s; parachutists fall from the sky; and soldiers fight mock battles. There are also naval displays.

Fireworks displays

One popular Independence Day tradition is fireworks demonstrations. In Israel, the custom dates back to 1950, when an Independence Day committee suggested a fireworks display to "create a suitable festive opening to Independence Day" and suggested combining the display with entertainment programs to liven things up even more.

The international Bible contest

Prizes for achievement in artistic, literary, and scientific areas are presented on Independence Day. Another popular tradition is the International Bible Quiz for Jewish Youth. The first quiz was held in 1958 in order to add religious meaning to the national holiday.

Foods, Recipes

Israelis are especially fond of picnicking and barbecuing on Independence Day. People get together with friends and relatives at the *mangal* (barbecue) and eat, drink, and have a good time. The most popular festival or street food during Israeli Independence Day is *falafel,* tiny croquettes made with chickpeas.

Music, Dance

The Israeli national anthem is called "HaTikvah," or "The Hope." It refers to the centuries-old hope for a unified Jewish homeland and that one day all exiled Jewish people will return to Israel.

> As long as a Jewish heart beats,
> and as long as Jewish eyes look east-
>   ward,
> then our two-thousand-year hope
> to be a free nation in Zion is not
>   dead.

Special Role of Children, Young Adults

A major traditional event on Independence Day is the International Bible Quiz for Jewish Youth. It is a fiercely competitive contest that is broadcast live on national television and attracts a large audience. First held in 1958, the contest is meant to bring spirituality to the holiday. It is so important to the nation that, in 1965, a member of the Israeli parliament asked the prime minister why no one from his office had escorted the winner, who was returning home to Australia, to the airport.

For More Information

Drucker, Malka. *The Family Treasury of Jewish Holidays.* Boston: Little, Brown, 1994.

Foy, Don. *Israel.* Milwaukee, Wis.: Gareth Stevens, 1997.

Web sites

"History of Israel." [Online] http://www.ahavat-israel.com/eretz/history.html (accessed on February 13, 2000).

"Remembrance Day/Independence Day." [Online] http://www.israel.org/mfa/go.asp?MFAH00y90 (accessed on February 13, 2000).

Mexico

Name of Holiday: Independence Day; Sixteenth of September

Introduction

A priest named Father Miguel Hidalgo y Costilla gave the poor people of Mexico the courage to rise up against Spanish rule when he gave the "Cry of Dolores" on September 16, 1810. This event marked the beginning of the Mexican War of Independence, which lasted until 1821. Today, the president of Mexico and city and town officials throughout the nation reenact Father Hidalgo's historic call to action on Mexican Independence Day.

History

In 1519, Spanish conquistadores (pronounced kahn-KEES-tuh-doors; conquerors), led by Hernando Cortés (1485–1547), arrived in the land that is now Mexico. They were searching for gold and were pleased to find the treasure-filled city of Tenochtitlán (pronounced tay-NOK-tee-TLAHN). Tenochtitlán was the main city of the Aztec Indians, and was built on the site of what is now Mexico City. The Spaniards destroyed the Aztec empire and claimed Mexico for Spain. Any Indians who resisted their rule were killed or enslaved.

By 1535, a Spanish governor had been appointed, and the territory had been named New Spain. By the end of the sixteenth century, this territory included most of what is now Mexico and Central America as well as a good portion of the southwestern United States. For the next three hundred years, the Spaniards prospered, and Spain reaped the benefits of goods and taxes collected from its new territory.

An unfair system of social classes

Under the caste system of New Spain, people were divided into social classes depending on their skin color and ancestry. At the top of the system were people born in Europe of pure Spanish blood. They were called the *gachupínes,* or "those who wear spurs." Next came the Creoles, who were people born in New Spain to Spanish parents. People of mixed Spanish and Indian or Spanish and black ancestry, called *mestizos,* were third. At the bottom of the social system were the native Indians and the blacks. The Spaniards had brought black slaves from Africa to work on their ranches.

This last group of people far outnumbered the Spanish and Creole population. They worked long hours with little reward. They owned no land, never had enough to eat, and remained poor and uneducated with no chance to better themselves.

Rumors of change in other lands

During the late 1700s, however, a spirit of revolution was in the air in much of the Western world. The American colonists were fighting for their independence from Great Britain, and the poor people of France struggled to put an end to the French monarchy and become a self-governing republic.

In New Spain, a few well-educated Creole priests had begun to write about the Spaniards' cruelty to the natives. Through these priests, New Spain's Indians, mestizos, and blacks learned they were not alone in their desire for independence from unjust rulers and for an end to social oppression.

Father Hidalgo: Friend of the native people

A Catholic priest named Miguel Hidalgo y Costilla (1753–1811), the son of Creole parents who managed a *hacienda,* or large ranch, played a critical role in the uprising of the Mexican natives and the declaration of independence from Spain. Hidalgo was so intelligent that his fellow students nicknamed him *El Zorro* ("the Fox"). He became a college teacher and priest during the late 1700s but resigned to become a parish priest in the small town of San Felipe.

Around 1800, Hidalgo was accused by other priests of reading "forbidden" books, and he lost his position in San Felipe. When his brother died in 1803, Hidalgo took over his post as priest in Dolores, a town located about 150 miles northwest of Mexico City. He ministered to the people and taught them to read. He also taught them how to tan hides, make good quality bricks and pottery, and grow trees and vines needed to produce silk and wine.

By order of the governor, these items could only be purchased directly from Spain. It was so expensive to buy them, that most people did without. When Spanish officials found out that Father Hidalgo was helping to make the poor people of New Spain more self-sufficient, they destroyed their crops and closed their businesses.

Like the French peasants before their revolution, the Mexican natives suffered from drought and food shortages. Families were near starvation, and there was no work for many men. Meanwhile, the privileged Spaniards grew more powerful and wealthy.

Father Hidalgo believed that all people should be free and equal. Angered by the government's actions against the people of Dolores, he continued to support the cause of New Spain's poor. Through reading and discussion with others, he became deeply involved in a movement for Mexican independence from Spanish rule. He even held meetings in his own home. During the fall of 1810, the people decided to revolt, setting December 8 as the date they would declare their independence. Spanish officials found out about the plan, however, which forced Father Hidalgo and his followers to act much sooner.

The Cry of Dolores

Late on the night of September 15 or early morning of September 16, 1810, Father Hidalgo rang the church bell, calling the people of Dolores together. He spoke to them about the taxation and tyranny of the Spanish government and the benefits of independence. Then he gave a yell to call the people to action, to declare their independence, and to be ready to fight for it. Although no one knows for certain what Father Hidalgo said, most accounts agree it was something like "Long live independence! Long live Mexico! Death to bad government!"

Father Miguel Hidalgo y Costilla, the father of the Mexican independence movement. Reproduced by permission of The Library of Congress.

The poor of New Spain echoed Father Hidalgo's words as he spoke them. This yell, given at the parish church in Dolores, is known as the Cry of Dolores. It began New Spain's eleven-year fight for freedom from Spain, and September 16 is the day that Mexicans celebrate as their Independence Day. Father Miguel Hidalgo is known as the Father of Mexican Independence.

Army or mob?

Learning of the revolution in Dolores, Indians, blacks, and mestizos came to the small town by the thousands, marching under the flag of the Virgin of Guadalupe (pronounced gwah-duhl-OOP), the religious symbol of New Spain's poor

The performance group Arte Andante acts out scenes from Mexico's struggle for independence on the streets of Mexico City on September 15, 1999, the day before Mexican Independence Day. Reproduced by permission of AP/Wide World Photos.

(see "Folklore, Legends, Stories"). Father Hidalgo and his captains soon led a spirited but untrained army of more than twenty thousand men, who were armed only with machetes, slings, knives, swords, and clubs.

They initially took over two towns, killing Spanish citizens and soldiers loyal to the Spanish Crown. More like an angry mob than an army, they also stole property and burned homes. The revolutionaries soon grew in number to as many as eighty thousand, and their wives and children joined the march to cook and care for the men. Many women even joined in the fighting.

Father Hidalgo soon earned the title of Generalísimo Hidalgo. The revolutionary fighters grew more violent in their rampages. At the city of Guanajuato, they killed Spanish soldiers and their wives and children who had barricaded themselves inside a fortress-like storehouse called the Alhóndiga. Then they looted and burned the town.

Hoping for an end to the war, Hidalgo outlined the desires of the Mexican people: an end to the caste system, equality for all Mexicans, an end to slavery, and an end to forced taxation of the poor. Hidalgo and revolutionary leaders who came after him also called for the redistribution of farmland to the common people of New Spain, who farmed the land for the wealthy but could not own it.

More and more priests joined Hidalgo and his revolutionaries, until about four hundred stood against the wealth and power of the Church's high officials. One of these priests was the mestizo Father José María Morelos y Pavón (1765–1815), a former student of Hidalgo's, who would soon prove his skill as a military leader.

By the end of October, the revolutionary army of eighty thousand had reached the capital, Mexico City. For some unknown reason, they did not attack. Some historians believe Hidalgo called off the attack because he feared his army would slaughter thousands of innocent people.

Hidalgo is captured, but fighting goes on

On March 21, 1811, Hidalgo and other leaders were captured by the Spanish while on their way to New Orleans, Louisiana, to seek the support of the United States for the revolutionary cause. Because Hidalgo was a priest, he could not be tried in court—only the Church could condemn him. He was declared no longer a priest and was executed on July 30, 1811, for treason. The heads of Hidalgo and others who were also convicted were displayed for several years at the Alhóndiga in Guanajuato.

The Mexican Revolution continued, with fighting erupting throughout New Spain. Revolutionaries fought in small bands, hiding and ambushing Spanish troops, then disappearing into the wilderness. In the south, Father Morelos, who proved to be a brilliant military leader, won many victories with his men.

New Spain declares independence

In November 1813, a congress called by Morelos declared New Spain's independence from Spain. Morelos was captured and executed in 1815, but the Mexican War for Independence continued, led by Nicolás Bravo (1786–1854), Vicente Guerrero (1783–1831), and Guadalupe Victoria (1789–1843).

Mexico wins freedom

In 1821, Agustín de Iturbide (pronounced ee-tur-BEE-day; 1783–1824), a Creole born in New Spain to a Spanish noble family, joined the fight for independence. He had been a soldier in the Spanish army fighting against the revolutionaries but decided to change sides. In February, he presented his "Plan of Iguala," which guaranteed three things to the people of New Spain: independence from Spain, with Mexico as an independent empire ruled by a member of Spain's royal family who lived in Mexico and followed its constitution; support for and protection of the Roman Catholic Church and its officials; and equal civil rights for everyone born in Mexico. These were called the Three Guarantees.

On August 24, 1821, Spain's representative signed the Treaty of Cordoba, recognizing Mexico as an independent nation. Six hundred thousand Mexicans had died fighting for independence since Father Hidalgo's Cry of Dolores in 1810.

Folklore, Legends, Stories

Many stories are told about the bravery of the common men and women who carried out the fight for Mexican independence in the early 1800s. Many legends also are connected to Mexico's fight for freedom. Here are two that are familiar to all Mexican schoolchildren who have studied the history of their country.

The brave "Chicken Neck"

Father Miguel Hidalgo led his army of mestizo farmers and Indians to take the city of Guanajuato shortly after the War of Independence began in 1810. When the city's Spanish soldiers and dignitaries saw the army approaching, they barricaded themselves, their riches, and their families inside a huge storehouse called the Alhóndiga. From inside this fortress, they fired on Hidalgo's army, killing wave after wave of attackers.

Hidalgo eventually asked for a volunteer to go up to the building and set fire to a large wooden door, which would allow the revolutionaries to get in. A young mine worker nicknamed *el Pipila* ("Chicken Neck") offered to do the dangerous job. He found a large, flat stone and tied it onto his back as a shield against the Spaniards' musket and artillery fire. Then, carrying a torch, he approached the building, crawled under the walls, and set the door on fire. When it burned through, the revolutionaries rushed inside, killing everyone they found in revenge for the two thousand men who lay dead outside the fortress.

The story of the Virgin of Guadalupe

In 1531, an Indian woodcutter named Juan Diego was on his way to mass early one morning when he saw a brown-skinned woman dressed in the clothing of the Indians of Mexico. She spoke to the woodcutter, telling him that she was the Virgin Mary, the mother of Jesus Christ. She instructed him to tell the local Catholic bishop to build a church in her honor on the spot where she appeared. The site was outside Mexico City, near the ruins of an Aztec temple for the goddess Tonatzin.

At first the bishop did not believe Diego and wanted proof that he had seen the Virgin. When the Virgin again appeared to Diego, she told him to cut some roses that she caused to grow nearby. He wrapped a bundle of them in his *serape* (pronounced seh-RAH-pay; blanket worn as a cloak). When Diego opened the blanket to show the roses to the bishop, an image of the Virgin was miraculously imprinted on the inside. The bishop ordered a church built on the hill where the Virgin appeared, and the blanket was framed in gold and displayed for worshipers.

The Virgin of Guadalupe, also called the Dark Madonna of the Hill of Tepeyac, was proclaimed Mexico's patron saint in 1737. Mexican revolutionary soldiers marched under a banner with her picture on it throughout the War for Independence, shouting "Long Live Our Lady of Guadalupe!"

Today, thousands of pilgrims journey to her church each year to thank her for answering their prayers. Many crawl up the hill to the shrine on their hands and knees. In 1976, a modern Basilica of the Virgin was built to replace the original church. Juan Diego's serape with the imprint of the Virgin on it is still displayed, now behind bulletproof glass, for the many visitors who come every day. The Basilica is the most visited Catholic religious site in the world after the Vatican in Rome, Italy.

Writers who influenced the Revolution

Father Miguel Hidalgo was a well-educated man who read the works of the great writers and philosophers of the seventeenth and eighteenth centuries, called the Age of Enlightenment. During the months before he gave the Cry of Dolores, Father Hidalgo often met with a group of intellectuals called the Querétaro Literary Club. This group discussed the ideas of these great thinkers as well as the political issues of the time in Mexico. At the heart of the discussions were the themes of self-rule and independence, and the motto of the French Revolution, "Liberty, Equality, Fraternity."

Customs, Traditions, Ceremonies

Independence Day celebrations in Mexico begin on September 15, with food, music, and dancing in the *zócalos* (pronounced SOH-cah-los), or central plazas, of towns all over Mexico. The festivities last until shortly before 11 P.M. At that time, a reenactment of the *Grito de Dolores* (Cry of Dolores) is presented in towns and villages throughout Mexico.

In Mexico City, the capital, where the nation's largest celebration is held, Mexico's president steps out onto the balcony of the National Palace and rings a replica of the historic cathedral bell rung in Dolores by Father Hidalgo in 1810. The palace overlooks a huge plaza where the Independence Day festivities are held.

At the last stroke of the bell, at exactly 11 P.M., the president gives the "Cry of Dolores," and the crowd echoes back the cry. The president's reenactment is recorded

Fireworks light up the sky above the Zocalo Plaza in Mexico City, Mexico, during Independence Day celebrations on September 15, 1999. Independence Day festivities include food, music, and dancing in the central plazas of towns all over Mexico. Reproduced by permission of AP/Wide World Photos.

live on national television. Afterward, confetti and the sound of party horns fill the air. Fireworks light up the sky with bursts of green, white, and red, Mexico's national colors. Music, dancing, and feasting go on until the early morning hours and continue the next day.

On Independence Day

On the Sixteenth of September, Father Hidalgo's picture is everywhere—on

Ballet Coco performs in downtown Los Angeles, California, September 11, 1999, during a three-day fiesta celebrating Mexican Independence Day. Reproduced by permission of AP/Wide World Photos.

posters and banners, in parades, at bull-fights, and in town squares. People make speeches to recall his leadership and his love for the common people of Mexico. Statues of the great leader are draped with garlands of flowers. In celebrations throughout Mexico, a young boy often portrays Father Hidalgo by dressing as a priest, while a young girl represents La Patria, or Mexico herself.

Independence Day bullfights are popular in some cities. Many people also attend rodeos, as they do in the United States on the Fourth of July. Others spend the day resting from work, because Independence Day is an official holiday.

Clothing, Costumes

In Mexico's larger cities, most people dress in Western-style clothing, but traditional costumes are worn for Independence Day and other festivals. For many of Mexico's festivals, women wear a blouse and skirt outfit called the *china poblana*, (pronounced CHEE-nuh poh-BLAH-nuh; "Chinese woman from Puebla").

According to legend, the outfit was introduced by a princess from India who was kidnaped by pirates and carried to Mexico as a slave. She became the servant of a wealthy couple of the town of Puebla.

Later in life she married a Chinese man, converted to Christianity, and performed many good deeds. She loved to wear a full, flounced red and green skirt trimmed in white lace with an embroidered white blouse and a silk shawl. The skirt was also decorated with sequins and beads.

Because she was well known for her kindness, the women of Mexico adopted her favorite outfit as their national dress. Mexican women and girls often wear the china poblana when they perform the Mexican Hat Dance, one of the country's most popular traditional dances.

At Independence Day and other fiestas, village women also wear *rebozos* (pronounced rree-BOH-sohs), which are long scarves that can also be used to carry a baby. Men wear *serapes* (pronounced seh-RAH-pays), colorful blankets worn wrapped around the body at night and thrown over the shoulder during the day. Mexican Indians make these in brightly colored weaves with designs that identify their home region.

Musicians wear tight-fitting suits with silver buttons and wide-brimmed hats. Rodeo performers wear beautifully embroidered shirts and pants. The men and women and their horses are decked out in silver, with their ornaments, buckles, knife handles, spurs, harnesses, and stirrups gleaming.

Mexican Hot Chocolate

Ingredients

1 teaspoon powdered cocoa

3 teaspoons sugar

1 mug hot milk

¼ teaspoon cinnamon

Directions

1. Mix cocoa, cinnamon, and sugar in a mug and fill it with hot milk, stirring well.

2. Top with a tablespoon of whipped cream or non-dairy topping. Serve with sugar cookies sprinkled with green, white, and red colored sugar. If you can find Mexican chocolate at a supermarket, melt a piece in a cup of hot milk. Pour the mixture into a large bowl and beat with a wire whisk until frothy. Mexicans use a wooden beater called a *molinillo*. Pour back into your cup and enjoy. Regular powdered cocoa can be used to make Mexican hot chocolate as well.

Foods, Recipes

Chiles en nogada (pronounced chih-lehs en noh-GAH-duh), Mexico's national dish, is always served at Independence Day fiestas. Meat-filled green chiles (hot peppers), red pomegranate seeds, and chopped parsley float in *nogada,* a creamy white sauce made from pounded walnuts and spices. The red, white, and green dish represents the colors of the Mexican flag. Sliced fruit, tacos, candies, and pastries called *churros* are other popular foods served on Independence Day.

Mexicans also love to celebrate Independence Day with a cup of hot chocolate, a favorite drink at any time of the year. The Aztec Indians drank hot

"Mexican National Anthem"

Mexicans, at the cry of battle
lend your swords and bridle;
and let the earth tremble at its center
upon the roar of the cannon.

Your forehead shall be girded, oh father-
      land, with olive garlands
by the divine archangel of peace,
For in heaven your eternal destiny
has been written by the hand of God.
But should a foreign enemy
Profane your land with his sole,
Think, beloved fatherland, that heaven
gave you a soldier in each son.

chocolate, which they made from cocoa beans that grow in Mexico.

Arts, Crafts, Games

The twentieth-century muralist Diego Rivera (1886–1957) is one of Mexico's best-known painters. Many of his murals detail Mexican history and the Indians of Mexico before the coming of the Spanish conquistadores. One of Rivera's famous murals depicts Father Hidalgo holding a torch and leading the common people into battle under the flag of Our Lady of Guadalupe.

Muralists José Clemente Orozco (1883–1949) and David Alfaro Siqueiros (1896–1974) painted great works on similar themes. They painted large murals in public buildings because they believed art should be seen by all people.

Folk art and toys at the bazaar

Mexican folk art and crafts are sold at open-air markets in every plaza throughout Mexico where Independence Day celebrations are held. The town squares are decorated with flags and flowers and lit with green, white, and red lights. Children may buy many kinds of toys painted in Mexico's national colors, as well as confetti, whistles, horns, and papier-mâché helmets.

Mexican rodeos and cowboys

One of the most popular events held on Mexican Independence Day are rodeos. Cowboys exhibit their horsemanship and ranching skills, such as roping, lassoing, and branding cattle. They also ride bulls and bucking broncos. Points are given according to the skill they show in performing each event. Women also perform at the rodeos.

Music, Dance

Mexico's national anthem is the "Himno Nacional Mexicano" ("Mexican National Anthem"), written during the mid-1800s, with lyrics by Francisco Gonzáles Bocanegra and music by Jaime Nunó (1824–1908). The hymn was first played on September 16, 1854, at the National Theater in Mexico City, when it was officially adopted as the national anthem.

A lively celebration of music and dance

Mexican Independence eve and day are filled with music and dancing. In the plazas, strolling *mariachi* bands entertain the crowd. Mariachi bands originated during the mid-1800s with the French occupation of Mexico, when small bands of musi-

A father and son watch balloons being released as part of the Mexican Independence Day celebration in downtown Los Angeles, California, September 16, 1996. Reproduced by permission of AP/Wide World Photos.

cians played for weddings and parties. Mariachi groups usually include two violins, two guitars, a large bass guitar, and a pair of trumpets, although they can have more than a dozen musicians. Mariachi songs are most often love songs sung in harmony.

Performances of Mexican folk dances and native Indian dances attract many visitors to town squares on Independence Day. The colorful costumes and feather headdresses of the Indian dancers and the Spanish-style or cowboy dress of the folk dancers add to the festive atmosphere. As music plays day and night, people dance in the square as they celebrate independence.

Special Role of Children, Young Adults

The celebration of Mexican Independence Day plays an important educational role for children in Mexico by helping to teach them about the history and people of their nation. Children march in parades and play the parts of historical figures such as Father Hidalgo and his military leaders in school pageants.

Aside from the history lessons, Mexican Independence Day is a joyous two-day celebration during which children join friends and families in the town square for delicious foods, music and dancing, and shopping for toys and gifts at the outdoor markets. They also may go to the rodeo, a bullfight or soccer game, a museum or amusement park, or a concert or play.

For More Information

The Mexican War of Independence. San Diego, Calif.: Lucent Books, 1997.

Stefoff, Rebecca. *Independence and Revolution in Mexico: 1810–1940.* New York: Facts On File, 1993.

Varona, Frank de. *Miguel Hidalgo y Costilla: Father of Mexican Independence.* Brookfield, Conn.: Millbrook Press, 1993.

Web sites

"Mexican Independence." [Online] http://www.tamu.edu/ccbn/dewitt/mexicanrev.htm (accessed on February 14, 2000).

"Mexicanos, Viva México!: Hidalgo's Call for Independence." [Online] http://www.mexonline.com/person1.htm/history.htm (accessed on February 14, 2000).

United States

Name of Holiday: Independence Day; Fourth of July

Introduction

During the 1700s, Americans who lived in the thirteen colonies under British rule grew weary of paying high taxes and having no voice in making the laws they lived by. On July 4, 1776, brave American leaders signed the Declaration of Independence in Philadelphia, Pennsylvania. In the years that followed, the colonists fought for and won their freedom in the American Revolution (1775–83). The Fourth of July is celebrated each year with fireworks and fanfare to commemorate the glory of the declaration of freedom.

History

Trouble between the thirteen American colonies and the British king, George III (1738–1820), started in 1764, when the king began taxing goods the American colonists bought from Great Britain. By paying these taxes, Americans were helping support the British Crown but had no voice, or representation, in making the British laws that affected the colonies. The British Parliament also passed acts that said Americans had to give room and board in their homes to British soldiers stationed in the colonies.

Men representing twelve of the thirteen colonies, all but Georgia, formed the Continental Congress, which met for the first time on September 5, 1774, in Philadelphia, Pennsylvania. The members agreed that the colonists should stop buying British goods if taxes were not lowered. People throughout the colonies had adopted the motto "No taxation without representation."

King George III did not lower taxes; instead, he sent more British soldiers to the colonies to enforce his laws. Americans formed militias (pronounced muh-LIH-shuz; citizens organized for military service), which trained "minutemen" to be ready to fight at a minute's notice.

In 1775, the British Parliament passed a law that said Americans could buy goods only from Britain. This angered the Americans even more, and fighting broke out between British soldiers and American minutemen on April 19. The battles of Lex-

Revolutionary minutemen, citizen soldiers ready to fight at a minute's notice, defended the American colonies against the well-equipped British army. Reproduced by permission of The Library of Congress.

ington and Concord, Massachusetts, followed, and American militia prepared to defend the colonies. The American Revolution had begun.

On May 10, 1775, John Hancock (1737–1793) was elected president of the Continental Congress. On June 16, George Washington (1732–1799) accepted the leadership of the Continental Army, which had been formed in Boston. The colonial government tried to make peace with Britain, but King George III refused.

The Continental Congress formed a navy, and some Americans met with leaders of other European countries to seek help in the war against Britain. France had lost its claim to land in North America to its old enemy, Great Britain, in the French and Indian War (1754–63). French leaders said they would consider helping the colonists win their freedom.

Declaring independence

In June 1776, colonial leaders Thomas Jefferson (1743–1826), John Adams (1735–1826), Benjamin Franklin (1706–1790), Robert R. Livingston (1746–1813), and Roger Sherman (1721–1793) were appointed by the Continental Congress to

The signing of the the Declaration of Independence as depicted by John Trumbull. If their bid for freedom failed, all the signers of the Declaration could have been hanged for treason. Reproduced by permission of the National Archives and Records Administration.

draft a statement saying that the colonies wanted to be free of British rule. The committee wrote down the ideas about freedom and self-government that had been discussed for the last several years in the various colonies. Thomas Jefferson, chosen for his writing skills, put these ideas together in a document called the Declaration of Independence.

On July 2, 1776, the Continental Congress met at the statehouse, later to be called Independence Hall, in Philadelphia, the seat of the colonial government. They read the Declaration of Independence, and representatives from each of the colonies voted for independence from Great Britain, creating the United States of America.

On July 4, 1776, after two days of discussing the declaration and making some changes, the men finally agreed that it was complete. John Hancock, president of the Continental Congress, signed the declaration, and copies of it were made and carried from town to town and state to state, where it was read to the people. It was also published in newspapers, and a copy was sent to King George III in England.

The most famous part of the Declaration of Independence is in the second paragraph: "We hold these truths to be self-evident, that all men are created equal, that they are endowed by their Creator with certain unalienable Rights, that among these are Life, Liberty, and the pursuit of Happiness."

Freedom worth fighting for

The signers of the Declaration of Independence knew that if their bid for freedom failed to bring independence they could all be hanged for treason against King George III. But they believed that freedom and self-government were worth the risk. Benjamin Franklin said, "We must all hang together, or assuredly we shall all hang separately." The first to sign the declaration, John Hancock, wrote his name in large, bold letters, saying, "His Majesty [King George III] can now read my name without spectacles [eyeglasses] and can double his reward ... for my head."

The American Revolution continued until 1781, when American soldiers and their French allies at sea won a major victory at Yorktown, Virginia. British General Charles Cornwallis (1738–1805) surrendered, and most of the fighting in the colonies stopped. By November 1782, American representatives Benjamin Franklin, John Adams, and John Jay (1745–1829) had negotiated a peace treaty with the British in Paris.

The treaty said that Great Britain would recognize the United States as an independent nation and withdraw all British troops. Britain also gave up its claims to land in eastern North America, expanding the United States to about twice the size of the original thirteen colonies. The Articles of Peace were approved by Congress on April 15, 1783, and the Treaty of Paris was signed on September 3 of that year.

The first Fourth of July celebration

In a letter to his wife, American statesman John Adams wrote that July 2, 1776, the day the Continental Congress voted in favor of a resolution declaring the colonies free and independent, should be celebrated by future generations. He suggested that it be remembered "as the day of deliverance, by solemn acts of devotion to God Almighty. It ought to be solemnized with pomp and parade, with shows, games, sports, guns, bells, bonfires, and illuminations from one end of this continent to the other, from this time forward evermore."

But the actual day of celebration became July 4, the day on which the Declaration of Independence was adopted and signed. Fourth of July celebrations have been held since 1777, beginning in Philadelphia, the first capital of the United States.

According to historical accounts, the first Fourth of July celebration included bonfires and fireworks. Bells rang, and ships in the harbor fired thirteen gun salutes, one for each colony. Congress took the day off, and members were treated to dinner and live music on board the warship *Delaware*. Throughout the city, people lit candles in their windows in the evening.

Other famous Fourths

As Philadelphia continued to celebrate the Fourth in a big way, each state began holding its own Fourth of July events. It became tradition to open newly constructed public buildings, monuments, war memorials, canals, railroads, and highways on the Fourth of July. Several new states were admitted to the union on the Fourth. The cornerstone was laid for the Washington Monument, Washington, D.C., on July 4, 1848. A copy of the Declaration of Independence is buried under the cornerstone.

The Declaration of Independence is based on the ideas that all people are creat-

Fireworks explode over the Washington Monument in Washington, D.C., on July 4, 1996. A copy of the Declaration of Independence is buried under its cornerstone. Reproduced by permission of AP/Wide World Photos.

In 1876, to celebrate the one-hundredth anniversary of the signing of the Declaration of Independence, Philadelphia held its Centennial Exposition. People came from all over the United States and from many nations throughout the world to visit the exposition and to celebrate. Alexander Graham Bell (1847–1922) introduced his new invention, the telephone. The gasoline engine and the typewriter were other inventions on display.

On July 4, 1885, the Statue of Liberty (*Liberty Enlightening the World*), by French sculptor Frederic-Auguste Bartholdi (1834–1904), was presented to the American people by the people of France to commemorate the signing of the Declaration of Independence.

During the United States' Bicentennial (two-hundredth birthday) Celebration on July 4, 1976, 212 ships sailed into New York Harbor from some thirty countries to salute the United States and the Statue of Liberty. The statue was repaired and restored during the mid-1980s, in time for an unveiling during a special Fourth of July celebration in 1986.

ed equal and are entitled to certain God-given rights. Throughout American history, groups that are fighting for such rights use the Fourth of July as a time to speak out. In 1876, Susan B. Anthony (1820–1906) and four other women made history when they handed out copies of the "Woman's Declaration of Rights" in the middle of Philadelphia's Fourth of July program at Independence Hall. They were working for "woman suffrage," or the right for women to vote in the United States.

Folklore, Legends, Stories

Countless stories and legends have been created to recount the heroics, sorrow, bravery, and passion connected to America's fight for independence. Some are as famous as the legend of the Liberty Bell; others may not be as well known, but are equally powerful.

Legend of the Liberty Bell

A legend about the Liberty Bell was first told in a book titled *Washington and*

His Generals, written by George Lippard in the mid-1800s. According to the story, an old man with "snow-white hair and sunburnt face" who served as the town bell ringer in Philadelphia, sat in the steeple of the statehouse on July 4, 1776, and awaited the outcome of the meeting in which the Continental Congress discussed the Declaration of Independence.

The old bell ringer told a young boy to wait in the hallway of the statehouse until a man gave him a message. The boy was then instructed to run out and shout the message up to the bell ringer. As John Hancock put his signature on the document, the boy ran into the street shouting, "Ring! Ring!" The old man rang the Liberty Bell with all his might to announce to Philadelphia that the colonies had declared themselves free.

During the American Revolution, as British soldiers advanced on Philadelphia, the Liberty Bell was removed from its tower and hidden in a church basement in Allentown, Pennsylvania, to keep it safe. In later years, the famous Liberty Bell was taken by train to many parts of the United States so that schoolchildren could see it. It is now on display in Independence Hall, Philadelphia, at the Independence National Historical Park. A picture of the Liberty Bell is also on the back of U.S. half-dollars.

Deaths of three patriots

One of the most remarkable Fourth of July stories is about Thomas Jefferson and John Adams, who were both on the committee that drafted the Declaration of Independence and both later served as presidents of the United States. The two men died on the same day—the Fourth of July—in 1826, exactly fifty years after the signing of the declaration. Jefferson died at his home, Monticello, in Virginia, and Adams at home in Quincy, Massachusetts. President James Monroe (1758–1831) died on the Fourth of July five years later.

Shortly before his death, Adams was asked to propose a toast for the upcoming Fourth of July celebration in Washington, D.C. He said, "It is my living sentiment, and by the blessing of God it shall be my dying sentiment—Independence now and independence forever!" It is said that Adams heard people in the street cheering "Independence forever!" as he died.

Customs, Traditions, Ceremonies

People in the United States celebrate Independence Day in much the same way as people in other countries. In cities and towns all over the United States, people watch fireworks displays, march in parades, listen to patriotic speeches, and enjoy picnics and outings. A special tradition is for new citizens to be granted citizenship on the Fourth of July.

Displays of sound and color

Boys began shooting fireworks to celebrate the Fourth of July during the 1800s. At that time, fireworks were unregulated, and large, dangerous firecrackers as well as play pistols that shot firecrackers were popular. Many boys were injured or killed, and every year sparks from Fourth of July fireworks started fires that destroyed houses, barns, and even whole towns.

A national campaign based on the slogan "Have a Safe and Sane Fourth" began in 1908. Many towns and cities banned fireworks within the city limits and replaced shooting fireworks with other activities, such as parades, historical plays and pageants, town picnics, sports and games, carnivals, and patriotic programs.

Today, most large cities hold spectacular fireworks displays that are regulated and safe. Every Fourth of July, thousands of people attend the events. In rural areas, setting off fireworks in the backyard is still a popular way to spend the Fourth.

Patriotism on parade

On the Fourth of July in 1788, a parade called "the Grand Federal Procession" was held in Philadelphia to celebrate not only independence but also the acceptance of the U.S. Constitution by ten of the thirteen states. Today, many patriotic groups march or ride on floats in Fourth of July parades, including military groups, marching bands, Boy Scouts and Girl Scouts, and veterans' organizations. Although Fourth of July parades are not held as often as they once were, many cities and towns carry on this tradition.

Fourth of July speeches

Speech making, or oration, became a Fourth of July tradition after a South Carolina patriot delivered the first speech in 1778. Each year, Fourth of July programs included stirring speeches about American history and the democratic form of government, the bravery of the founding fathers, and the growth and progress of the nation.

Some of America's most famous speakers began by giving Fourth of July addresses, including John Quincy Adams (1767–1848), the sixth U.S. president, and Daniel Webster (1782–1852), lawyer and statesman. The Fourth of July is still a popular time for political candidates to kick off campaigns for office and for those in office to address the people they represent.

Picnics, outings, rodeos, and races

As American cities grew, formal Fourth of July celebrations decreased, and people began to celebrate the Fourth by going on picnics and family outings. Those living in larger cities along rivers were able to take day-long steamboat rides, perhaps with live music on board, and see a fireworks display over the water. Others took a train trip to the countryside or stayed in the city and went to the circus or zoo.

Going on such outings is still the way most people spend the Fourth of July, much like the French do on Bastille Day and the Israelis on their Independence Day. Families may take summer vacations the week of the Fourth and go to a favorite park or vacation spot to swim, camp, fish, or canoe. Or they might go home for a family reunion.

Many spend the day going to a museum, a movie, out to dinner, and then to watch a fireworks display at night. Others cook hot dogs and hamburgers in the park, play softball or volleyball, or sit on a blanket to enjoy an outdoor concert. Some participate in watermelon-eating and seed-spitting contests.

In the western and southwestern states, some towns hold rodeos on the Fourth of July, featuring bull riding and roping, barrel racing, bronco riding, and other contests. Prizes are given for the best cowboy or cowgirl in each category.

New citizens

Each year on the Fourth of July, dozens of new American citizens take the oath of citizenship in Arlington, Virginia, at Freedom Park. The practice of granting citizenship on the Fourth of July began in 1915 with Americanization Day in several cities, and has continued as a way of reinforcing patriotism among new American citizens.

Foods, Recipes

Since the early 1800s, people have gathered on the Fourth for outdoor feasts. If the weather prevented this, they met in taverns, hotels, public buildings, or in someone's home. Most outdoor meetings were held in parks or on the lawns of colleges, churches, or other public buildings. Usually the gathering were held under the shade of trees and near a spring or river to help celebrants keep cool on the hot July days.

Today, Fourth of July cookouts with hot dogs, hamburgers, or barbequed chicken, pork, or beef are the most popular way to share a meal. Fried chicken is also a favorite, especially in the South. Clambakes are popular in New England. Trimmings for a cookout include roasted potatoes or corn on the cob, potato salad or cole slaw, baked beans, deviled eggs, pickles, hot peppers, and onions. Lemonade, watermelon, and homemade ice cream are other Fourth of July treats.

Arts, Crafts, Games

Probably the most famous work of art about the American Revolution is *The Spirit of '76* (originally called *Yankee Doodle*), by American painter Archibald Willard (1836–1918). It was first viewed by the public during the Centennial Exposition in Philadelphia on America's one-hundredth birthday in 1876, and was displayed in art

Grilled Corn on the Cob

1. Carefully pull husks all the way back from ears of fresh corn, but do not pull them off.
2. Wash the ears, removing the corn silk. Fold the husks back over the corn, and tie the husks closed around the top of the ears with a strip of husk or string.
3. Soak the ears of corn in water for about 1 hour to help keep the husks from burning on the grill.
4. Grill over a medium-low fire for about 20 minutes. Serve with butter and salt and pepper.

museums throughout the United States in the months following the celebration.

Willard is said to have first painted it as a humorous picture to show a Fourth of July parade in a small town. He changed the painting to represent three generations of Americans, a boy and his father and grandfather, marching off to fight in the American Revolution. A 13-year-old boy named Henry Devereaux posed as the drummer boy in the picture. The famous painting is now displayed in Marblehead, Massachusetts.

"Uncle Sam"

The drawing of the stern, bearded man in the tall hat and red, white, and blue coat with a finger pointed directly at the viewer was based on a real man, Samuel Wilson, who supplied meat to the U.S. Army

Fourth of July Firecracker Costume

If your school or neighborhood has a Fourth of July parade, you can easily make a firecracker costume to wear. Staple together two large sheets of red, yellow, or blue poster board. Form them into a tube to fit around your body by stapling the ends together. Wear shorts in the same color or in another bright color.

Make a headband out of heavy construction paper and attach one end of a sparkly or glitter-covered pipe cleaner to the band. Bend the pipe cleaner so that it curves from the top of your head and then stands up like a firecracker fuse. March in the parade with the cardboard tube around you, your fingers holding up the bottom of the tube.

during the War of 1812. Wilson put the initials U.S., for United States, on the barrels of meat he shipped to the army. Soldiers began saying the initials stood for Uncle Sam, and before long, "U.S." and "Uncle Sam" became one and the same. New York cartoonist Thomas Nast drew the character during the late 1800s, and James Montgomery Flagg portrayed Uncle Sam on a famous Army recruiting poster for World War I (1914–18).

Music, Dance

Outdoor concerts featuring various types of music are held today on the Fourth of July. Marches are especially popular for Independence Day celebrations. Russian composer Pyotr Tchaikovsky's *1812 Overture,* punctuated by cannon fire and clashing cymbals, has become the musical signature for the Fourth of July.

"Yankee Doodle"

The song "Yankee Doodle" became popular as early as 1775, when fighting first broke out between the British uniformed soldiers, often called "Red Coats," and the colonial militia, who were farmers, craftsmen, and laborers who volunteered to fight. The Americans had no real uniforms when they went into battle, and the British sang this song to make fun of their ragged, mismatched clothes.

> Yankee Doodle went to town
> a-riding on his pony.
> He stuck a feather in his cap
> And called it macaroni.
>
> Yankee Doodle, keep it up.
> Yankee Doodle dandy.
> Mind the music and the step
> And with the girls be handy.

But when the colonials won the battle at Concord, Massachusetts, early in the American Revolution, they adopted "Yankee Doodle" as their anthem, proud of the common men's victory over the well-trained British soldiers. General George Washington's Continental Army often whistled the song or played it on the fife (a type of wooden flute) and drum as they marched into battle.

When the Americans won the war after the battle of Yorktown, "Yankee Doodle" was one of the songs played to celebrate the victory. It was also played on the first Fourth of July celebration in 1777 and has become a traditional patriotic song played during Fourth of July parades and programs each year.

"The Star-Spangled Banner"

"The Star-Spangled Banner" is the national anthem of the United States. It was originally written as a poem, titled "Defence of Fort M'Henry," by Francis Scott Key (1779–1843) during the War of 1812 (1812–14). It was 1814, and Fort McHenry in Baltimore, Maryland, was under attack by the British. Key, a lawyer on a war-related mission, watched from on board a ship as British cannon and rocket fire bombarded the fort throughout the night.

When dawn broke, the American flag—the "star-spangled banner"—was still flying over the fort as a sign that the Americans had not surrendered. Inspired by their bravery and the sight of the flag waving "by the dawn's early light," Key wrote the words to what would become his country's national anthem in 1931. His poem was set to music from a song by John Stafford Smith called "To Anacreon in Heaven" and renamed "The Star-Spangled Banner."

"The Star-Spangled Banner"

Oh, say can you see by the dawn's early light

What so proudly we hailed at the twilight's last gleaming,

Whose broad stripes and bright stars through the perilous fight

O'er the ramparts we watched were so gallantly streaming?

And the rockets' red glare, the bombs bursting in air,

Gave proof through the night that our flag was still there.

Oh say, does that star-spangled banner yet wave

O'er the land of the free and the home of the brave?

For More Information

Giblin, James Cross. *Fireworks, Picnics and Flags.* New York: Houghton Mifflin, 1983.

Sandak, Cass R. *Patriotic Holidays.* New York: Crestwood House, 1990.

Web sites

"Archiving Early America: Historic Documents from 18th Century America." http://www.earlyamerica.com (accessed on February 1, 2000).

Independence Hall Association. "ushistory.org: the Congress of Websites." [Online] http://www.ushistory.org (accessed on February 14, 2000).

Independence Day Sources

Albyn, Carole Lisa, and Lois Sinaiko Webb. *The Multicultural Cookbook for Students.* Phoenix, Ariz.: Oryx Press, 1993, pp. 30–33.

Appelbaum, Diana Karter. *The Glorious Fourth: An American Holiday, An American History.* New York: Facts On File, 1989, pp. 54–58, 75–113, 155–58, 170–72.

Banfield, Susan. *The Rights of Man, The Reign of Terror: The Story of the French Revolution.* New York: J. B. Lippincott, 1989, pp. 88–90, 133–37, 156–58, 167–69, 177, 196–99.

Brace, Steve. *Ghana.* New York: Thomson Learning, 1995, pp. 4, 20, 23, 44.

Gilbert, Adrian. *The French Revolution.* New York: Thomson Learning, 1995, pp. 6–39.

Goodwin, William. *Mexico.* San Diego, Calif.: Lucent Books, 1999, pp. 41–45, 52–53, 89–93.

Greene, Gloria Kaufer. *The Jewish Holiday Cookbook.* New York: Times Books, 1985, pp. 287–89.

MacMillan, Dianne M. *Mexican Independence Day and Cinco de Mayo*. Springfield, N.J.: Enslow, 1997.

Penner, Lucille Recht. *Celebration: The Story of American Holidays*. New York: Macmillan, 1993, pp. 15–21.

Reilly, Mary Jo. *Mexico*. New York: Marshall Cavendish, 1994, pp. 48–49, 84, 88–91, 100–101, 103–07.

Shillington, Kevin. *Independence in Africa*. Austin, Tex.: Raintree Steck-Vaughn, 1998, pp. 40–41, 45, 57–58.

Travers, Len. *Celebrating the Fourth: Independence Day and the Rites of Nationalism in the Early Republic*. Amherst: University of Massachusetts Press, 1997, pp. 73–83, 220–22.

Winter, Dave, and John Matthews. *Israel Handbook*. Chicago: Passport Books, 1998, pp. 29–44.

Wylen, Stephen M. *The Book of the Jewish Year*. New York: UAHC Press, pp. 119–30.

Web sites

Garbrah, Steve. "Nana Yaa Asantewaa of the Ashanti Empire." [Online] http://www.ashanti.com.au/nana.htm (accessed on February 13, 2000).

"The Golden Stool of the Asante Nation: A Symbol of Unity and Leadership." [Online] http://www.ashanti.com.au/ashhis.htm (accessed on February 13, 2000).

Mogues, Tseguereda. "14 July—A National Holiday in France." [Online] http://www.larocheind.com/bastil.htm (accessed on February 14, 2000).

"Music in Ghana: An Overview." [Online] http://www.ghana.africaonline.com/Africa-Online/covermusic.html (accessed on February 14, 2000).

"Recipes from Ghana." [Online] http://www.sas.upenn.edu/African_Studies/Miscellany/Recipes_from_12913.html (accessed on February 14, 2000).

"Remembrance Day/Independence Day." [Online] http://www.israel.org (accessed on February 14, 2000).

"Time Line—America During the Age of Revolution, 1764–1775; 1776—1789." [Online] http://lcweb2.loc.gov/ammem/bdsds/timelin2.html (accessed on February 14, 2000).

Kwanzaa

Introduction

Kwanzaa (pronounced KWON-zuh) was created as a new holiday in 1966 by Maulana Karenga (1941–), an author, black leader, and professor of black studies at California State University. Karenga worked during the Black Liberation Movement of the 1960s to make sure that African Americans received the same rights as white citizens of the United States. He formed an organization called Us (or US), based on rules of conduct called "the Seven Principles." Karenga then created Kwanzaa as a way to promote African culture and heritage and to bring African Americans together to better their lives, families, and communities.

History

Many of the symbols and ceremonies of Kwanzaa come from African "first fruits of the harvest" celebrations dating from as far back as ancient Egypt and continuing up through modern African harvest celebrations like Nigeria's New Yam Festival and Swaziland's Incwala, or First Fruits Festival. Kwanzaa also borrows customs from other African peoples, including the Ashanti and Zulu.

The extra *a*

The name Kwanzaa comes from *matunda ya kwanza*, which means "the first fruits" in Swahili (pronounced swah-HEE-lee), the language spoken by a majority of African people. An extra *a* was added to the end of *kwanza*, meaning "first fruits," which gave the holiday seven letters to match the Seven Principles on which it is based.

According to Maulana Karenga, the holiday's founder, at the first Kwanzaa celebration there were seven children who each wanted to represent a letter of Kwanzaa in a play. At that time, the new holiday was still called Kwanza, with only six letters. An extra *a* was added to the end of the word for the seventh child.

A growing celebration

At first only a few hundred blacks in the United States celebrated Kwanzaa, but over the years the celebration grew rapidly. It also became popular with black families in South America, the Caribbean, and throughout the world. One source esti-

Holiday Fact Box: Kwanzaa

Themes

Celebrating the African American family, community, and cultural roots; bringing African Americans together to better their lives, families, and communities; giving thanks for the earth's bounty and for the good in life.

Type of Holiday

Kwanzaa is a cultural holiday for people of African descent. It is a secular holiday that is not associated with any particular religion, and is celebrated by people of all faiths. It is meant to be celebrated in addition to—not instead of—Christmas or any other religious holiday.

When Celebrated

Kwanzaa is celebrated during the seven-day period from December 26 through January 1, but it is said to continue throughout the year as people put the Seven Principles of Kwanzaa into practice in their daily lives.

mates that Kwanzaa is celebrated today by between eighteen and twenty million people worldwide.

In 1996, the thirtieth anniversary of Kwanzaa, the U.S. Postal Service created a special Kwanzaa postage stamp. Museums, community centers, and other organizations in several cities hold Kwanzaa marketplaces or cultural exhibits in late December to help celebrate the holiday.

Folklore, Legends, Stories

Some of the ideas and proverbs on which Kwanzaa is based come from a sacred book of the Yoruba people of Nigeria. This sacred book is called the *Odu of Ifa*. In this book, an ancient wise man named Orunmila says, "Surely, humans were chosen to bring good into the world." He also says that each person must take responsibility for helping create a good life in a safe, peaceful, and happy world. This takes strength and good character and a desire to help those in need. It also takes a lifetime commitment to working for the kind of beautiful world in which people deserve to live.

Folktales for Kwanzaa

People who celebrate Kwanzaa can choose from hundreds of African, Brazilian, or Caribbean folktales to help them learn about their heritage and to illustrate the Seven Principles. In Africa, storytellers and musicians who were the keepers of the ancient folktales and tribal histories were called *griots* (pronounced GREE-ohz).

In the early days of slavery in the American colonies, the United States, and the Caribbean, the griots kept the slaves' African heritage alive by passing these stories on. Many of them have been written down and preserved and retold by modern writers. Among the most well known are the stories about Anansi, the Spider, from the Ashanti people of Africa.

Customs, Traditions, Ceremonies

On each of the seven days of Kwanzaa, a special ceremony is performed based on which of the Seven Principles is being

The Seven Principles

Unity

"Unity," or *umoja* (pronounced oo-MOH-jah), refers to the oneness of family, community, nation, and all people of African descent. It is celebrated on the first day of Kwanzaa, December 26.

Self-determination

The second principle is self-determination, known as *kujichagulia* (pronounced koo-jee-chah-goo-LEE-ah). This principle encourages blacks to speak for themselves, to set their own goals, to define who they are as persons of African descent, and to decide who they want to be in life. It is celebrated on the second day of Kwanzaa, December 27.

Collective Work and Responsibility

"Collective work and responsibility," or *ujima* (pronounced oo-JEE-mah), is about working together as a community to solve one another's problems and to build and maintain the African community itself. It is celebrated on the third day of Kwanzaa, December 28.

Cooperative Economics

The fourth principle of "Cooperative Economics," known as *ujamaa* (pronounced oo-jah-MAH-ah), encourages African Americans and the Pan-African community to establish their own shops and businesses and, in earning a living through them, to help all black people to prosper. It is celebrated on the fourth day of Kwanzaa, December 29.

Purpose

"Purpose," or *nia* (pronounced NEE-ah), encourages black people to work together to build, develop, and defend the black community, to save its culture and history, and to add to the good and beauty in the world. It is celebrated on the fifth day of Kwanzaa, December 30.

Creativity

"Creativity," known as *kuumba* (pronounced koo-OOM-bah), encourages black people to use their creativity to make the community where they live—and the world—more beautiful and helpful than it was when they were born into it. It is celebrated on the sixth day of Kwanzaa, December 31.

Faith

The seventh principle, called *imani* (pronounced ee-MAH-nee), is about having faith in all black people—in parents, teachers, and leaders—and believing that the struggle to regain the greatness of the African people is right and will be successful. It is celebrated on the final day of Kwanzaa, January 1.

Sacred Duty (A Poem for Ujamaa)

The sound
of an ancient horn echoes
from our past, the call to the
sacred duty
of true nation building.
Arise and unite,
you well minded
able bodied children
of Mother Africa scattered
all over the world,
use the divine gifts of
talent so bountifully bestowed
upon you to help all our people
create communities
where genuine freedom
and justice reign supreme.
Go Forth.
Be fruitful
in every
positive way
to fill each
and every corner
of our beautiful planet
with abundant life,
love,
beauty,
everlasting joy.

—*Sami Bentil*

Source: Dorothy Winbush Riley. The Complete Kwanzaa: Celebrating Our Cultural Harvest. *New York: HarperCollins, 1995, p. 154.*

that holds the seven candles of Kwanzaa, and the unity cup.

At the beginning of each ceremony, family members greet one another with the question, "Habari gani?," which is Swahili for "What news?" They answer with the name of the principle being celebrated on that day. For example, they would respond, "Umoja" on the first day of Kwanzaa and "Kujichagulia" on the second day.

Each evening's ceremony is usually closed with a special blessing, such as, "Tonight and all nights, we celebrate the spirits of all those who are here with us. Tonight and all nights, we celebrate the spirits of those who are yet to come."

Pouring tambiko

On each of the seven nights of Kwanzaa, a ceremony called *tambiko* (pronounced tahm-BEE-koh) is held to honor the ancestors. An elder of the family pours water or juice from the ceremonial unity cup into a large bowl of fresh lettuce or other greens. The liquid is poured from the four directions—north, south, east, and west.

As the elder pours, he or she makes a tambiko statement, which honors the ancestors, calling some of them by name. The ancestors are people of ancient Africa, black people in this and other centuries who have worked to improve the lives of their people, and family members of previous generations who have died.

Then the elder takes a sip from the unity cup and passes it first to the other elders in the family, to the parents, and finally to the children, until everyone has taken a sip. In very large gatherings, only the elder performing the tambiko takes a sip.

celebrated. The ceremonies, held in the evenings in individual family homes, are centered around such Kwanzaa symbols as the *kinara,* a seven-branched candleholder

"Harambee!"

After the elder has taken a sip from the unity cup during the tambiko ritual, or at any time during Kwanzaa, the family or group may join in shouting "Harambee!" (pronounced hah-RAHM-bay), an African word meaning "Let's all pull together!" It is usually shouted seven times for the Seven Principles. As they shout, people hold their right arms high with the hand open and then pull downward, making a fist. This call to collective work and unity began with the organization Us during the 1960s.

Lighting the candles

After the tambiko ritual, one person in the family or group lights the candle that stands for the particular day's principle, beginning with the black candle of unity on December 26, the first day of Kwanzaa. Children are especially encouraged to participate in the candle lighting.

The person who lights the candle names and explains the principle of the day. Then the family discusses the principle and people, living and dead, who have represented that principle during their lives. They might begin with a statement like, "We celebrate the spirits of all those who understood that all children of Mother Africa share a common heritage and a common destiny."

After the first day of Kwanzaa, the candles are lit each day, alternating between red and green, beginning with the first red candle on the left in the kinara. This symbolizes that struggle, represented by red, must always come before a prosperous future, represented by green. After the candle for each day of Kwanzaa is lit, the ones that were lit on previous days of Kwanzaa are re-lit, so that all seven candles are burning by the last day of Kwanzaa. The candle lighting ceremonies of Kwanzaa are similar to those of the Jewish holiday Hanukkah, when eight candles are lit in a special candleholder called a *menorah* (pronounced muh-NORE-uh).

The community feast

On December 31, the sixth day of Kwanzaa, a community celebration called a *karamu* (pronounced kah-RAH-moo) is held. This is a feast of African, Caribbean, Latin American, and African American foods, with every family bringing a special dish.

The hall or community center where the karamu is held is decorated in the Kwanzaa colors of black, red, and green. All the food is placed on a large mat, and everyone serves themselves. Tambiko is offered, and the Seven Principles are discussed. There may also be programs with singing and dancing. The karamu is a joyful community gathering that is followed the next day by quiet times and gift giving.

The farewell statement

A farewell statement, or *tamshi la tutuaonana* (pronounced TOM-shee lah too-too-ah-oh-NAH-nah), written by Kwanzaa founder Maulana Karenga, is used to close out the karamu and the year and to renew commitment to the Seven Principles during the coming year:

> Strive for discipline, dedication and achievement in all you do. Dare struggle and sacrifice and gain the strength that comes from this. Build where you are and dare leave a legacy that will last as long as the sun shines and the water flows. Practice daily Umoja, Kujichagulia, Ujima, Ujamaa, Nia, Kuumba and Imani. And may the wisdom of the ancestors always walk with us. May the year's end meet us

Participants singing a hymn at the annual Kwanzaa candlelighting ceremony in Los Angeles, California, in 1995. Kwanzaa ceremonies center around the kinara and its candles, the unity cup, and the other Kwanzaa symbols. Reproduced by permission of AP/Wide World Photos.

laughing and stronger. May our children honor us by following our example in love and struggle. And at the end of next year, may we sit again together, in larger numbers, with greater achievement and closer to liberation and a higher level of human life.

After this statement is read, everyone joins in calling "Harambee!" seven times.

A day for thinking about things

On January 1, the last day of Kwanzaa, everyone takes time to look back over the past year and think about his or her life and how he or she might improve it in the future. This is also a time to decide what can be done to make the family and the community better in the months to come. As with New Year's Day in other societies, taking a day to think about life and how to improve it in the coming year is a tradition among many African tribes.

Kwanzaa wishes

African Americans wish one another a "Happy Kwanzaa" or, in Swahili, "Kwanzaa yenu iwe na heri" (pronounced KWON-zah YAY-noo EE-way nah HAY-ree), or "heri" for short. In recent years, commercially made Kwanzaa cards have been available to buy and send, although many people prefer to make their own.

Clothing, Costumes

Because Kwanzaa is a time for celebrating all things African, many people wear African style clothing during the holiday. This clothing is made from brightly colored cotton cloth with bold patterns and designs. Women and girls often wear long dresses or belted robes. To complete the African costume, they wear matching head wraps.

Men and boys sometimes wear a shirt or a long, loose robe called a *kanza*. These are worn over loose-fitting, lightweight pants. People who do not have a traditional African costume may wear whatever colorful clothing they have, with matching hair ornaments, scarves, or hats and perhaps beads or pendants made from natural materials.

Foods, Recipes

The Kwanzaa karamu, or "feast," is a time when African American or Pan-African communities come together and celebrate the wonderful heritage of foods that come from Africa, the Caribbean, and parts of Latin America, as well as from the days of slavery in North America. A meal with these traditional foods may also be served at home during each of the other six nights of Kwanzaa.

When whole communities join in preparing food for the karamu, at least five of the Seven Principles of Kwanzaa are used: unity, collective work and responsibility, cooperative economics, purpose, and

creativity. Eating and helping prepare the foods of the ancestors helps children learn about African culture and teaches them to pass these ways on to their own children in the future.

Soul food

Between the 1500s and the 1800s, African men, women, and children were brought to the American colonies as slaves. For the voyage, slave traders often stocked their ships with foods from Africa that the people were accustomed to eating, such as yams, various fruits, nuts, and beans. In America, the slaves were able to cultivate some of these foods. They also ate whatever they grew on the plantations as well as game they killed and fish they were able to catch.

Corn was a staple food in the American colonies, and cornmeal mush and cornbread became everyday foods for the slaves. Wild greens were plentiful, as were fish and shellfish in the coastal areas. Ham, bacon, and pork from hogs slaughtered on the plantations also made up a part of the slaves' diet. The ham, shrimp, and rice dish called jambalaya is often served at Kwanzaa karamus, because it was a popular dish among blacks living along the Gulf of Mexico.

The foods and style of cooking that grew up around slavery in America are known as "soul food," and these simple dishes are always found at a karamu. A few of the soul food dishes are hoppin' John, a spicy dish made from black-eyed peas, sausage, and rice; sweet potato pone, a pudding made from shredded sweet potatoes with pineapple, coconut, and raisins; peach cobbler; potato salad; collard greens; cornbread; fried green tomatoes; stewed okra and tomatoes; and fried chicken.

Hoppin' John

Ingredients

1 pound black-eyed peas

½ pound salt pork

1 pound sausage or turkey

4 cups cooked long-grain brown rice

1 large onion, chopped

4 cloves garlic, crushed

1 large bay leaf

2 teaspoons dried oregano

2 teaspoons dried basil

1½ teaspoons salt

½ teaspoon cayenne pepper

Directions

1. Pick out any stones or discolored black-eyed peas, then wash the peas thoroughly. Soak them overnight, then drain them and put them in a large pot.

2. Cover the peas with fresh water. Add onion, garlic, and bay leaf. Bring to a boil, then turn heat to low and cook for about 1 hour, until almost done. Stir occasionally and add water if needed as peas cook.

3. Fry salt pork and sausage or turkey in a separate pan, pour off excess fat, and cut sausage or turkey into bite-size pieces. Add cayenne pepper and mix well.

4. Add meat, salt, and herbs and cook until peas are completely done and flavors are well mixed. Serve over rice.

Serves approximately 4

African, Caribbean, and Brazilian flavors

The many cultures that make up Africa today all have their own styles of cooking and favorite foods, any of which may be served during Kwanzaa. A few African dishes are baked mealies (corn) and tomatoes; curried rice with raisins and nuts; chicken and groundnut (peanut) stew; beef curry; peanut and beef gumbo; chicken cooked in coconut milk; rice with lamb; yams and squash; chickpea (garbanzo bean) salad; fried plantains (a sort of banana); groundnut truffles (peanut candy); and fish with cumin (a spice).

African people were also taken to the Caribbean Islands as slaves to work on sugarcane and other plantations. Many foods popular in the Caribbean today were introduced by the African slaves and so are prepared for Kwanzaa. Some of these are sweet potato fried bread; coconut spinach; meat and beans cooked with plantains and coconut milk; spinach stew; curried lamb or goat; jerk pork or chicken; and rice and black-eyed peas.

South America's largest country, Brazil, has many people of African origin who were also taken to that country as slaves. Brazil's national dish, *feijoada* (pronounced fay-hoe-AH-dah), is a stew made from various meats, black beans, and tomatoes, served with rice. Mixed greens and black-eyed pea fritters are also popular dishes that may be prepared for Kwanzaa.

Arts, Crafts, Games

One of the most engaging aspects of Kwanzaa is its emphasis on creating crafts and works of art based on African motifs and traditions, rather than using store-bought items. These items—such as greeting cards, gifts, and decorations—are central to celebrating the holiday. According to the creator of Kwanzaa, Maulana Karenga, to reinforce the ideals and purpose of the holiday everyone should follow the principle of creativity (kuumba), and make as many items by hand as possible.

Decorating for Kwanzaa

Kwanzaa decorations are created along African themes and are predominantly in the colors of Kwanzaa—black, red, and green. Most decorations are made of natural materials, such as straw or wood. The centerpiece for Kwanzaa celebrations is a table on which holiday symbols are arranged. A brightly patterned African cloth is placed over the Kwanzaa table, and a *mkeka* (pronounced mm-KEY-kay), or mat, is placed on top. The mat represents African tradition and history. Symbols of Kwanzaa, including fresh fruits and vegetables and ears of corn, are placed on and around the mkeka. Green plants also add to the beauty of the natural celebration.

Making a Family Mkeka

A project a family might want to try during Kwanzaa is to make their own *mkeka.* Have each family member design a square that represents one or more of the Seven Principles. One suggestion is to sew together scraps of clothing that recall special memories, such as squares or shapes cut from a daughter's first dress. This mini "quilt of memories" serves as a reminder that a family is united. When each square is finished, they can all be sewn onto a background cloth to make a mkeka for use at next year's Kwanzaa. The family mkeka may also become a treasured keepsake for years to come.

Symbols

Seven Principles, seven symbols, seven candles, seven letters in Kwanzaa, seven days of celebration—the number seven was chosen to represent Kwanzaa because it is considered a sacred number in many of the world's religions and cultures, including those of Africa. African harvest festivals often lasted either seven or nine days. According to Maulana Karenga, the number seven is also a good number for teaching and learning new ideas.

First fruits symbols

Seven special symbols based on traditional African festivals that honor the first fruits of the harvest are used in the celebration of Kwanzaa. All Kwanzaa symbols should be made from natural materials.

Mkeka: A straw or cloth mkeka, or mat, is a symbol that history and tradition are foundations on which to build a good life, just as the present is built on the past. In ancient Africa, mats were woven from dried stalks of grain. Today, families buy mats made of straw or of cloth made in Africa. The six other Kwanzaa symbols are placed on the mat.

Mazao: *Mazao* (pronounced mah-ZAH-oh; crops), or fruits, nuts, and vegetables, are placed in a bowl made of natural materials, like straw, wood, or clay. They are the symbols of African villagers working together to grow and harvest food for the community, for which all members are thankful. For Kwanzaa, the mazao represents work and responsibility to family and community members.

Muhindi: *Muhindi* (pronounced moo-HIN-dee) are ears of corn that represent each child in the family. Children are symbols of the family's future and are also linked to the past through their ancestors. In African tribal villages, every adult helped care for the children, so the people of Nigeria have a saying that "It takes a whole village to raise a child."

On Kwanzaa, people show love and caring not only for their own children but for all the children of their community, especially those who are homeless or hungry. If there are no children in the family, at least one ear of corn should still be placed on the mkeka to represent the possibility of children as well as the community of children for which everyone is responsible.

Mishumaa saba: The *mishumaa saba* (pronounced mee-SHOO-mah SAH-bah), or

seven candles—three red, three green, and one black—represent the Seven Principles, or *nguzo saba* (pronounced en-GOO-zoh SAH-bah), of Kwanzaa. The black candle represents the principle of unity; the three red candles stand for the principles of self-determination, cooperative economics, and creativity; and the three green candles represent the principles of purpose, collective work, and faith. Each principle is celebrated on a different day of Kwanzaa. Beginning with the black candle of unity, one candle is lit on each of the seven days.

Kinara: A seven-branched candleholder holds the seven candles of Kwanzaa. The candleholder, called the *kinara* (pronounced kee-NAH-rah), must be made from natural materials, such as wood or clay. A sturdy piece of bark or driftwood may serve well as a kinara. The shape does not matter, as long as there are seven separate spaces for the seven candles. The black unity candle should be placed in the center, with the three green candles placed to the right and the three red ones to the left.

The kinara represents the family's African ancestors, who, in spirit, are said to look after the living family members. It is based on the Zulu story of Nkulunkulu, the First Born, who is represented by the symbol of a corn stalk.

Kikombe cha umoja: The cup of unity is called the *kikombe cha umoja* (pronounced kee-KOME-bay chah oo-MOE-jah). It is the ceremonial cup everyone drinks from during the Kwanzaa ritual known as the tambiko, which means "spiritual offering." A special drink is reserved for the ancestors, and the eldest member of the family or community says a special blessing.

The unity cup ceremony comes from African rituals in which liquids are offered to the ancestors as a sign of worship and respect. The Ibo people of Nigeria believe the last drink of an offering belongs to the ancestors and will bring bad luck to any living person who consumes it.

Zawadi: Family members give children gifts, or zawadi (pronounced zah-WAH-dee), usually on the last day of Kwanzaa. These are very often handmade and educational and are usually on an African theme. Shopping for expensive gifts does not have a place in Kwanzaa. Zawadi should have meaning and should teach children something or encourage self-determination and success. They should also make children smile.

Zawadi are given by parents to children to show their love, and to reward children for some accomplishment or for keeping promises. Books, especially on African subjects, and African heritage symbols are almost always given to children during Kwanzaa, along with African games, dolls, clothing, paintings, or posters. Families might also make cards or gifts for guests they plan to entertain during Kwanzaa. Giving a gift to someone makes him or her part of the family.

The Kwanzaa flag

A special Kwanzaa flag was designed using the colors of the organization Us: black, red, and green. These colors were named the colors for Africans all over the world by Marcus Garvey (1887–1940), a Jamaican who worked for human rights and economic self-sufficiency for black people in the United States.

Called the Bendera (pronounced bayn-DAY-rah), the Kwanzaa flag has a black stripe, a red stripe, and a green stripe. The black stripe stands for all black people; the red is for the blood of the ancestors and the continuing struggle for freedom and equality; and the green represents the land and the fruits of the harvest, the future of black people, and the hope that comes from hard work.

Music, Dance

Playing native African instruments, especially drums, and dancing are an important part of African festivals and are often included in Kwanzaa celebrations. People might learn traditional African folksongs as well. Songs, music, and dance are performed during the karamu, or community celebration, and family members may give musical performances on any night of Kwanzaa.

As the holiday has grown in popularity, new music has been created especially for Kwanzaa. Musicians Steve Cobb and Chavunduka recorded the first Kwanzaa compact disc and cassette in 1993. Called *The Seven Principles,* it includes a song for each day of Kwanzaa, plus a song they released in 1992 called "It's Kwanzaa Time."

Special Role of Children, Young Adults

Children play an important part in all Kwanzaa activities, especially in the lighting of the seven candles. Children also make Kwanzaa decorations, help prepare certain foods, and make Kwanzaa cards and small gifts for guests. Encouraging children to learn about their African heritage is a main principle behind Kwanzaa, because children are the future of the community and must pass on their heritage to bring about unity.

Chi Wara (right), the antelope that represents the new year, dances to traditional music during Kwanzaa festivities in Los Angeles, California, in 1997. Playing native African instruments, especially drums, and dancing are often a part of Kwanzaa celebrations.
Reproduced by permission of AP/Wide World Photos.

Kwanzaa programs

Children often put on special programs for Kwanzaa that may feature traditional African songs, dances, plays, readings from African folktales, or stories about famous African Americans. They might organize short programs to present to their families on each night of Kwanzaa or plan programs for the Kwanzaa karamu, or feast, on the sixth night. In some communities, children have their own karamus, held at schools or churches or at a child's home.

Serving the community

Many black families organize or participate in special community projects during Kwanzaa, in which children are included. For example, to show the principle of collective work and responsibility (ujima), the family might participate in a program to take food or blankets to a homeless shelter, visit hospital patients, or present a play for senior citizens. Activities such as these take place not only during Kwanzaa, they are also held throughout the year to keep alive the spirit of the Seven Principles.

Receiving zawadi

Receiving gifts, or zawadi, is a special activity for children during Kwanzaa. Zawadi are more meaningful than gifts a child might receive for Christmas or a birthday. They are meant to reward and educate children and are often handmade by parents or other relatives—except for books, which are always given for Kwanzaa.

A heritage symbol is also given and can be an African figurine or design, either bought or handmade; a drawing or painting; or a framed photograph of a famous African or African American. Zawadi are always accompanied by a few special, and often humorous, words about why they hold a special meaning for the child. When the child accepts the gift, he or she is making a promise to fulfill the spirit of the gift.

For More Information

Karenga, Maulana. *Kwanzaa: A Celebration of Family, Community and Culture.* Los Angeles: University of Sankore Press, 1998.

Riley, Dorothy Winbush. *The Complete Kwanzaa: Celebrating Our Cultural Harvest.* New York: HarperCollins, 1995.

Walton, Darwin McBeth. *Kwanzaa: World of Holidays.* Austin, Tex.: Raintree Steck-Vaughn, 1998.

Web sites

"Happy Kwanzaa." (representing Canada's black community) [Online] http://www1.sympatico.ca/Features/Kwanzaa (accessed on February 21, 2000).

"Kwanzaa Information Center." [Online] http://www.melanet.com/kwanzaa (accessed on February 21, 2000).

"Official Kwanzaa Website." (affiliated with Maulana Karenga) [Online] http://www.OfficialKwanzaaWebsite.org (accessed on February 21, 2000).

Kwanzaa Sources

Copage, Eric V. *Kwanzaa: An African-American Celebration of Culture and Cooking.* New York: Quill, 1993.

Harris, Jessica B. *A Kwanzaa Keepsake: Celebrating the Holiday with New Traditions and Feasts.* New York: Simon & Schuster, 1995, pp. 31, 67.

Karenga, Maulana. *Kwanzaa: A Celebration of Family, Community and Culture.* Los Angeles: University of Sankore Press, 1998.

Riley, Dorothy Winbush. *The Complete Kwanzaa: Celebrating Our Cultural Harvest.* New York: HarperCollins, 1995, pp. 20–27, 154.

Thompson, Sue Ellen, ed. *Holiday Symbols 1998.* Detroit, Mich.: Omnigraphics, 1998, pp. 222–26.

Webb, Lois Sinaiko. *Holidays of the World Cookbook for Students.* Phoenix, Ariz.: Oryx Press, 1995, pp. 3–44, 203–13, 228–30.

Web sites

"First Kwanzaa CD Released." [Online] http://www.ltskwanzaatime.com/music.html (accessed on February 20, 2000).

"What Is Kwanzaa?" [Online] http://www.melanet.com/kwanzaa/whatis.html#TOC (accessed on February 20, 2000).

Index

Italic type indicates volume numbers;
boldface type indicates entries and their page numbers;
(ill.) indicates illustrations;
(box) indicates information found in sidebar boxes.

Index

China poblana *3:* 263, 306, 309
China *1:* 2, *2:* 209–14, *4:* 347–61
Chinatowns *4:* 358
Chinatown (Yokohama, Japan) *4:* 349 (ill.)
Chinese New Year *4:* 347–61
Chinese tiger *1:* 23 (ill.)
Chinese Zodiac *4:* 351 (box), 356
Ching Ming Festival *2:* 209–14, 211 (box), *4:* 370
Christmas *1:* **69–135**, 71 (ill.), 76 (ill.) 81 (ill.), 83 (ill.), 86 (ill.), 89 (ill.), 91 (ill.), 93 (ill.), 97 (ill.), 99 (ill.), 102 (ill.), 105 (ill.), 106 (ill.), 111 (ill.), 122 (ill.), 124 (ill.), 126 (ill.), 130 (ill.), *3:* 322, 331–33, *4:* 362, 366, 371, 378, 392, 403, 418
Christmas cards *1:* 77
A Christmas Carol 1: 73, 74
Christmas concert *1:* 124 (ill.)
Christmas Cranberry Bread (recipe) *1:* 125
Christmas Eve Torchlight Parade *1:* 126 (ill.)
Christmas markets *1:* 83 (ill.)
Christmas Seals Campaign *1:* 79 (box)
Christmas trees *1:* 70
Church bells *2:* 144, 171
Church of San Jorge (Roha, Ethiopia) *1:* 91 (ill.)
Church of Scotland *4:* 391
Circumambulation *1:* 9
Clothes *2:* 142, 147, 180, 202, 212, 216, 228, *3:* 327, *4:* 358, 365, 410
Clowns *1:* 23, 37–38, 37 (ill.), 47
Cocoa *3:* 281, 308
Cofradías *2:* 178, 183
Coins *4:* 366, 372, 375, 400
Colcannon (recipe) *2:* 231
Cold Food Day *2:* 210
Cole, Henry *1:* 78
Collop Monday *1:* 16
Cologne *1:* 35–36, 36 (ill.), 39
Colombia *2:* 153–61
Colombian Corn Soup (recipe) *2:* 159
Colored eggs *4:* 340, 344, 375, 378
Columbus, Christopher *1:* 117, *4:* 434
Commedia dell'arte *1:* 24, 47
Comus *1:* 59
Concentration camps *3:* 247 (box), 292
Confetti *1:* 42
Confucius *2:* 209
Constantine the Great *2:* 142, 161, *3:* 290
Constantinople *2:* 161, 169
Constitutional monarchy *3:* 273
Continental Congress *3:* 270, 310-13
Convention People's Party *3:* 281
Coptic Christian Church *1:* 90
Coptics *1:* 90, 93 (ill.)

Cornbread Turkey Dressing (recipe) *4:* 472
Cornucopia *4:* 433, 472
Cortés, Hernando *3:* 299
Costaleros *2:* 178
Costumes *1:* 17, 20, 26, 28, 29, 39, 43, 47, 50, 51, 54, 62, 64, *2:* 180, 196, 200, 202, 208, 216, 222, 229–30, 233, 237, 238, *3:* 262, 274, 306, *4:* 356, 358, 371
Council of Nicaea *2:* 139, 161
Count Dracula *2:* 207
Coup d'état *3:* 284
Cowbellion de Rakin Society *1:* 58
Crafts *2:* 204, *3:* 308, 329, *4:* 360, 378, 399
Crane, Ichabod *2:* 235 (ill.)
Crèche 1: 84
Creoles *3:* 300–03
Cristes mæsse *1:* 70
Cry of Dolores *3:* 258, 262, 301, 303, 305
Czech Republic *4:* 435–39
Czestochowa, Poland *2:* 169

D

Dalian, China *4:* 357 (ill.)
Dance *1:* 25, 62, 88, *2:* 208, 217, *3:* 331, *4:* 397
Darius the Great *4:* 335, 372
David *3:* 267, 288, 290, 295 (ill.)
David, Jacques–Louis *3:* 264, 277
Day of Atonement *4:* 379
Day of the Dead *2:* 195, 211, 217, 218–26
Days of Awe *4:* 386
Declaration of Independence *3:* 258, 311-14, 312 (ill.)
Declaration of the Rights of Man and of the Citizen *3:* 257, 270, 273
Decorations *1:* 83, *2:* 207, 217, 223, 236, 238, *3:* 331, *4:* 343, 352
Ded Moroz *1:* 87
Denmark *1:* 109
Despedimiento *2:* 156
Devil's Night Fires *2:* 237 (box)
Dharma *1:* 1, 3
Dharma wheel *1:* 12
Diaspora *3:* 289
Dickens, Charles *1:* 73
Dinh Bang, Vietnam *4:* 346 (ill.)
Dipas *4:* 362, 364, 366, 370 (box), 371
Disciples *2:* 138, 141, 143
Divination *2:* 196, *4:* 373, 394
Diwali *4:* 335, 341, 345, 361–71, 390
Diwali lamps *4:* 340, 366, 370